MINISTRY O
AGRICULTURE, FISHERI

C000150958

An ABC
of
Home Freezing

Bulletin 2 1 4

LONDON
HER MAJESTY'S STATIONERY OFFICE

HER MAJESTY'S STATIONERY OFFICE

Government Bookshops

49 High Holborn, London WC1V 6HB
13a Castle Street, Edinburgh EH2 3AR
41 The Hayes, Cardiff CF1 1JW
Brazennose Street, Manchester M60 8AS
Southey House, Wine Street, Bristol BS1 2BQ
258 Broad Street, Birmingham B1 2HE
80 Chichester Street, Belfast BT1 4JY
*Government publications are also available
through booksellers*

ISBN 0 11 241114 2

Contents

Preface

Some 3,000,000 freezers were estimated to be in use in the UK in 1975. The figure is likely to be higher for 1976, but it still leaves a large proportion of the population without freezing equipment. For those among them who may be considering investing in it, this book gives a thorough practical guide to home freezing. It is based on extensive scientific experimentation carried out over many years in the Ministry of Agriculture, Fisheries and Food's own unit at Long Ashton Research Station, which is directly concerned with Home Food Storage and Preservation. In other words, it offers to the potential buyer of a freezer the chance to ask himself or herself, Do I really want a freezer, and What do I expect to get out of it? It summarizes all the information available that will enable him or her to answer those questions.

A freezer is a great asset in the home if it is used properly. Possibly it may achieve only marginal savings in money, but what may not be obtained in substantial savings will be more than balanced by the advantages of constant availability of high quality food, from an appliance which is here for the foreseeable future. These advantages are in the food itself, in savings of time, money and convenience, and they are summarized below.

A. FOOD

1. Food quality and nutritional value

The freezing process retains more of the original eating quality and nutrients than any other domestic preservation method.

2. Safety

Frozen foods held at −18°C (0°F) or below present no health hazard. Care is needed during the pre-freezing and thawing periods when the food is as perishable as similar fresh food.

3. Range of food

A greater variety of foods can be preserved by freezing than by any other method. The range covers fresh or cooked primary foods such as fruit, vegetables and meat, plus baked goods and complete meals.

4. Choice

Gluts of seasonal crops can soon lose their attraction. With a freezer, excess good quality produce can be frozen for use throughout the year.

5. Quantity/portions

Portions can be adjusted to suit your personal needs.

6. *Preparation and utilization*

Usually preparation time is no longer than for food to be eaten fresh. Most vegetables have to be blanched before freezing but this has the advantage of reducing the final cooking time.

7. *'Doubling-up'*

In many recipes it is easy to handle double or treble the quantities which could be used freshly prepared. Immediate requirements can then be met and the remainder frozen for future use.

C. MONEY SAVING

8. *Bulk buying*

Bulk purchase of favourably priced good quality food can be frozen for use over the coming months. With constantly rising prices savings can be effected.

9. *Catering packs*

Purchase of large sized packs can offer a definite saving.

D. CONVENIENCE

10. Food can be prepared ahead for special occasions or to give a break from routine meal preparation.
11. Visits to shops can be reduced. The handicapped and elderly can particularly benefit by choosing quiet periods and good weather for shopping.
12. Those living alone can avoid the embarrassment of a shortage of food when unexpected visitors arrive.
13. Full-time workers can avoid or minimize late shopping when some foods may be sold out.
14. A sudden call due to an emergency can be met from a well-stocked freezer.

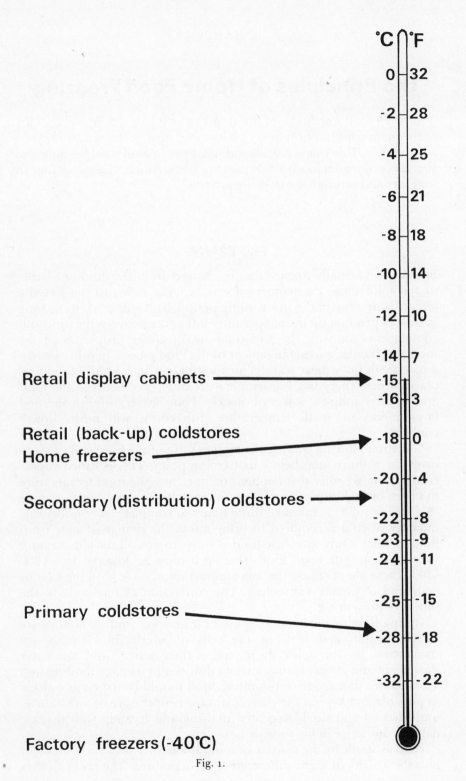

Fig. 1.

CHAPTER 1

The Principles of Home Food Freezing

THE AIM of all methods of food preservation is to process it for subsequent consumption in such a way that quality changes are kept to a minimum. This chapter deals with the principles of food freezing and the safety of frozen foods while they are being frozen, during storage in a freezer and through the thawing process.

FREEZING

Before food actually freezes, that is, changes from the fluid or pliable to the solid state, the temperature is brought down to the freezing temperature zone in the pre-cooling period. This will be short or long in time depending on the temperature difference between the food and cooling environment, the particular heat transfer properties of the food and the size and arrangement of the food pieces. In other words, a food with good heat transfer properties, cut into small pieces and placed where there is a big temperature difference between the food and its surroundings, will cool quickly. Poor heat transfer properties, large pieces or small temperature differences, will mean slower cooling.

Sometimes during cooling the temperature of the food continues to drop for a short time below its freezing point. This is called super-cooling, but whether this happens or not, once the food temperature has been brought down to the freezing zone it will soon start to change to a frozen solid. It can take some hours to complete. A considerable quantity of cold is required to bring about the change of state from fluid to solid. Only when the food is truly frozen will the temperature start to drop. For good food freezing it must be lowered to $-18°C$ ($0°F$). These are of course the same temperature: $-18°$ is on the Celsius scale and $0°$ on the Fahrenheit. The conversion of one scale to the other is shown in Fig 1.

During freezing pure water separates from food, and ice crystals are formed within and between the cells of which food tissues are composed. Ice occupies more space than water, and so water movement and crystal formation can distort and damage food tissues. To keep this damage to a minimum, food should be frozen as quickly as possible and kept at the correct storage temperature of $-18°C$ ($0°F$) until thawed and used. Repeated thawing and freezing will increase damage due to ice in the food tissues.

Food is spoilt by the activity of natural enzymes present in all cells, plus the activity of many different micro-organisms. The faster food is

4

frozen the sooner is this spoilage slowed to a minimum. Most micro-organisms are completely inactive once the food reaches −10°C (14°F). Enzymes function so slowly at the recommended frozen food storage temperature of −18°C (0°F) that food has the high quality storage life that we expect from foods preserved in this way.

THE STORAGE OF FROZEN FOODS

Stored frozen foods do not remain unchanged. Their colour, texture and flavour alter very slowly until they are unacceptable. The rate of this change depends on the temperature at which the food is stored, the quality of the food at the point of freezing, which in turn is affected by the way that it is handled before freezing, and the characteristics associated with particular foods. When stored at the correct temperature of −18°C (0°F), most fruits and vegetables will remain acceptable for 12 months, joints of meat from 6−12 months and bread for 3 months. Foods that store successfully for 12 months at −18°C can be unacceptable after 2 months at −10°C (14°F). Deterioration between −10°C and −18°C is due to the slow working of enzymes which brings about changes in flavour, texture and colour. If the temperature of storage rises above −10°C there will also be growth of spoilage bacteria which will increase progressively the higher the temperature. Bacteria causing illness (pathogens) if present in food will *not* grow until food has completely thawed.

THE THAWING OF FROZEN FOODS

There is still a lot to learn about the changes which occur during the thawing of frozen foods. As thawing occurs, the temperature will rise to where the solid frozen food changes to a pliable or fluid consistency. This is the same temperature zone as for freezing, but the reverse change of state can take even longer than freezing. Water is a poorer conductor of heat than ice and once a film of water forms around a thawing food particle, the particle is to some extent insulated by this water layer, thus reducing the rate of further thawing. Whatever the method of thawing, the smaller the pieces of frozen food and the greater the temperature difference between the food and its surroundings the faster it will thaw.

If a food is perishable before it is frozen it is at least as perishable, and possibly more so, when removed from the freezer, and it should be treated as such. Do not be over-worried about micro-organisms and frozen foods. The efficient thawing and cooking of frozen food as a combined process or a sequence will ensure the safety and quality of frozen foods. As soon as the temperature of food gets above about −10°C (14°F) some spoilage bacteria will start to grow, although very slowly, but before any significant microbial growth can occur, properly handled food will have been thawed out and utilised.

Cooking kills most micro-organisms, but thawed foods should not be left for any length of time before cooking, even at refrigerator temperatures. The cooked food should then be cooled as quickly as possible to reduce microbial spoilage to a minimum. These are the well-understood rules of safety and hygiene in the kitchen.

THE MICROBIOLOGY OF FROZEN FOODS

All fresh foods contain micro-organisms which may be naturally present or acquired during harvesting, slaughter and subsequent handling. The micro-organisms comprise the bacteria, yeasts and moulds. They can be a costly nuisance as many micro-organisms spoil foodstuffs and are a major cause of food wastage. Apart from the activities of the spoilage organisms which make food unsightly and unpalatable, harmful organisms causing illness can multiply on food. Spoilage and hazardous micro-organisms may be present on the food we set aside for freezing.

As the temperature of the food is lowered the activity of the contaminating micro-organisms is slowed down.

Freezing and frozen storage does not destroy many of the micro-organisms in food. Some are killed but many simply become dormant, ready to grow again when the temperature is raised. With very few exceptions, such as one form of *Cl. botulinum,* pathogenic bacteria cannot grow at refrigerator temperatures 2–4°C (35–40°F). For the limited storage life possible at this temperature, foods are generally safe.

The spoilage micro-organisms are more tolerant of low temperatures and spoilage moulds, yeasts and bacteria can grow down to about −10°C (14°F) or even lower. However, it must be stressed that micro-organisms cannot grow at the recommended running temperature of the home freezer of −18°C (0°F) and no hazard to health or microbial spoilage will occur during storage at this temperature. But if mishandling prior to freezing has allowed large numbers of micro-organisms to grow and produce toxins, freezing will not rectify this dangerous situation. Considerable heat has to be absorbed to change ice into water. If foods such as meat and poultry are inadequately thawed before cooking, protecting layers of ice may still surround some micro-organisms and cooking may fail to destroy them. These can subsequently multiply and may cause illness if this food is later eaten cold. Post-freezer preparation for the table must ensure destruction of micro-organisms and any left-overs must be handled hygienically to eliminate any health hazard.

THE NUTRITIONAL VALUE OF FROZEN FOODS

The freezing process has been called a truly gentle method in terms of the preservation of nutrients.

THE EFFECT OF FREEZING AND FROZEN STORAGE ON THE NUTRIENT CONTENT OF FOOD. Almost all the significant effect is due to pre-freezing operations such as blanching and the post-freezing thawing and cooking. It should be kept in mind that some loss of nutrients is inevitable in any food unless it is eaten in prime condition fresh from its source. The necessary transport and storage chain followed by preparation and, perhaps, cooking and serving will reduce some nutrients and this reduction can be severe where handling methods are poor.

EFFECTS OF DELAY BEFORE FREEZING. The home producer has the opportunity to use really fresh fruit and vegetables without delay and 'pick it yourself' facilities can be almost as good if the produce is kept cool and covered during the journey home and then quickly utilized. Green vegetables held at 15°–21°C (60°–70°F) may lose 15% of their ascorbic acid (vitamin C) content per day, especially if they are bruised, packed in deep boxes or exposed to draught. Other vegetables and soft fruits are subject to similar but smaller losses. Where washing to remove dirt is necessary it should be done quickly, as prolonged soaking leads to loss of soluble nutrients. Similarly, any trimming or chopping, dicing or slicing should be done in the sequence of preparation for freezing, not in advance.

All the above factors apply to primary foods regardless of final use. The changes which ultimately lead to deterioration in the taste, flavour and nutrient content of stored foods are reduced at low temperatures; the specific causes of nutrient losses in frozen foods arise from the specialised techniques of preparation and utilization or from the process itself and its duration and these are considered in greater detail in the sections which follow. In general, the nutrients in frozen foods are well retained and when foods in prime condition are prepared and frozen properly, stored at −18°C (0°F) or lower for not longer than the recommended time, and treated correctly on removal from the freezer, differences between the nutrient content of cooked fresh and cooked frozen foods on the plate will be small.

PREPARATION LOSSES. Certain foods will discolour any lose palatability during frozen storage unless given a pre-treatment to inactivate the enzymes causing these changes. Blanching or scalding in hot water is commonly used for most vegetables and some fruits as the heat destroys the enzymes, but inevitably small amounts of some minerals and water soluble vitamins dissolve in the water and are lost. Steam blanching is less destructive of soluble nutrients but is impracticable in the home. Losses in hot water blanching can be minimised by careful attention to quantities and timing, and by serial use of the same blanching water 6 or 7 times. Blanching in fast boiling water for a short period causes smaller nutrient losses than the use of simmering water for a longer period. It should be possible to keep ascorbic acid loss down to 5–10% (depending on type of vegetable) but this can increase to 70% with careless untimed blanching. The cooling period after blanching should also be carefully timed to prevent further leaching of nutrients. The pH of the blanching water can affect the amount of thiamin (vitamin B_1) present because this vitamin is more easily destroyed by heat in alkaline (hard) water.

Blanching also has the advantage of displacing the air in the plant tissues. Oxygen in the air and within the food itself can cause changes which lead to losses of some nutrients during storage. In vegetables oxidative changes can be controlled by blanching but other means must be found to retard the browning which occurs in light-coloured fruits such as peaches and pears. The addition of ascorbic acid to the syrup before freezing prevents this reaction of the oxidative enzymes, and it is likely that the overall ascorbic acid content of the frozen product will also be increased. Moreover, since the syrup is usually consumed with the fruit, any leached nutrients are not lost. The exclusion of air when packing for freezing (see p. 34) is also of considerable importance in reducing nutrient losses.

THE FREEZING PROCESS. The faster the freezing rate the better for nutrient retention and food quality in general but some physical damage of tissue by ice crystal formation is inevitable. Fluctuations in the temperature of food in the freezer also damage the cells and give rise to drip of the cell contents on thawing and thus to a loss of soluble nutrients if the drip is not used. Apart from this the freezing process itself does not affect the nutritional value of foods. Some proteins may be affected at freezer temperatures, for example, the albumen in the white of hard-boiled egg toughens excessively. There are a number of other minor nutritional changes due to the effects of freezing and low temperatures but these are beyond the scope of this Bulletin.

STORAGE. The recommended maximum frozen storage period for a food is determined by its organoleptic acceptability and it has been found that good eating quality generally indicates good retention of the original nutrients as well.

In fruits and vegetables, vitamins A and C and thiamin may be partially destroyed if storage conditions are unsatisfactory or the temperature rises above −18°C (0°F). The ultimate loss of ascorbic acid depends on the length and temperature of storage.

A comparison between matching pairs of blanched and unblanched vegetables in frozen storage showed an initially higher ascorbic acid content in the unblanched samples, but this dropped throughout storage so that after 4–6 months the amount in the blanched material, which had largely retained its initial ascorbic acid, was higher and this advantage increased as storage was prolonged. The loss of ascorbic acid linked with loss of eating quality.

In fatty foods, particularly meat and fatty fish, there is a tendency for oxidative rancidity to develop and any vitamin A present will be destroyed; such foods cannot therefore be stored for long periods at −18°C (0°F). The presence of salt in foods such as bacon accelerates oxidation. Rancidity is easily detected at an early stage by tasting; domestically the only deterrent is very careful packing to exclude air.

UTILIZATION. Most vegetables are cooked from the frozen condition and retain their nutrients well provided that they are cooked in a closed saucepan in relatively little water. The double heating of vegetables, i.e. blanching and subsequent cooking, does not double the loss of vitamin C because the initial blanching generally reduces the loss in subsequent cooking and a shorter cooking time is required. However, losses can be very heavy if either process is prolonged. Once the food is ready to serve, any delay before eating should be minimised, as a significant loss of vitamin C can occur in cooked vegetables in as short a time as 10 minutes.

When fruit is frozen for subsequent jam-making, quick heating from the frozen condition is advised and, as with fresh fruit, copper pans must be avoided because of the destructive effect of the metal on ascorbic acid.

The nutritional value of home-frozen food prepared in the recommended way will compare very favourably with foods frozen by commercial methods, especially where for large scale operations rather damaging techniques, such as mechanical pea podding, have to be used.

POINTS TO NOTE FOR RETENTION OF NUTRITIONAL VALUE OF FROZEN FOODS

1. Select high quality fresh produce.
2. Store for minimum period before freezing, preferably use at once.
3. Keep produce cool and handle quickly, avoiding prolonged soaking.
4. Blanch efficiently, using the same water for consecutive batches or use other appropriate treatment to reduce deteriorative enzyme action where necessary.
5. Wrap to exclude air, and prevent dehydration and oxidation.
6. Freeze immediately.
7. Hold at steady freezer temperature.
8. Use within recommended storage period.
9. Thaw wrapped and preferably slowly at low temperatures or cook from frozen where appropriate.
10. Utilize drip containing soluble nutrients.
11. Eat as soon as possible.

CHAPTER 2

Economics of Food Freezing at Home

APART FROM the cost of the food, four main factors determine the cost of freezing food in the home.

1. Cost of the freezer.
2. Miscellaneous costs: Insurance, repairs, utensils and freezer accessories, eg thermometer, books.
3. Packaging material eg containers, freezer bags, etc.
4. The cost of electricity.

THE FREEZER

Capital outlay, ie the initial cost of the freezer. Freezers are available over a wide range of prices and a considerable discount can be obtained on most models; so it is sensible to obtain a lot of freezer prices to find out the least money that has to be spent to get the freezer you want. To give some guidance, a 14·0 cu. ft. (400 litre) chest freezer costs about £180·00 and a 4·0 cu. ft. (110 litre) upright £120·00 (September 1977). Upright freezers and refrigerator freezers cost more to buy than chest freezers of equivalent capacity and tend to cost more to operate as well.

A large freezer will cost less per cubic foot of space it provides to buy, than a small freezer, but its operating costs will be higher particularly if it is half empty or the food in it is not densely packed (air is a bad conductor of cold). Whichever model you buy, if you keep it for the ten-year life or more you can expect from a freezer, the operating costs over this period will be much greater than the initial cost.

Although we do not usually consider depreciation and loss of income on capital when buying domestic appliances they should be borne in mind. A freezer loses much of its value during the first year or two of its use and much less per year towards the end of its life. It is therefore important to buy a freezer which is going to suit your requirements for some years, as frequent purchase of new models makes the cost of home freezing very expensive. If you are buying a freezer to save money on food, your total food costs must be consistently 10–20% below those you would have without a freezer. Buying too large a freezer for your needs, with high operating costs, will make it impossible to keep food costs down.

The interest on capital is the money that would have been earned in interest, if the money spent on buying the freezer had been invested instead, Depreciation plus the interest on capital can be up to £1·00 a week for a large freezer and about 50p a week for a moderately sized model, again assuming a ten-year life for the freezer.

MISCELLANEOUS COSTS

Many of these costs can be avoided but not spending money on them can lead to high operating costs, poor quality food from the freezer and considerable financial loss.

These costs include money spent on:–

(a) Utensils such as blanching and bag sealing equipment; (b) alarm systems to indicate power failure or a dangerous rise in temperature; (c) thermometers to ensure the freezer is running at the correct temperature of –18°C; (d) insurance; (e) an allowance for spare parts and repairs; (f) books including the record books so important for managing the freezer economically and for withdrawing food within its high quality life. Some of these costs occur once only, but £30–50 can be easily spent in this way, plus a sum of £10–15 per year to cover insurance, repairs, etc.

PACKAGING

If 120 gauge 'use once' plastic bags are bought at 1000 rates, packaging will cost about 0·3p per lb of food. However, these bags do not stand rough handling and therefore the stronger 150 gauge bags may be preferred. These, at 1000 rate, cost about 0·4p per lb of food; if gussetted they enable a squarer, space saving pack to be formed. Tight packing not only saves space in the freezer but also cuts down electricity costs per pound of food.

Waxed cartons cost about 4p per lb of food; if re-used five times, this reduces their cost to 0·66p per lb. However, if re-used it is advisable to line them with a plastic bag which increases the cost again. A high initial expenditure on plastic cartons can be justified in terms of the ease of handling and sealing, their value in protecting fragile foods and the fact that good quality plastic containers will last a long time.· Cheaper plastic containers will not withstand repeated use at low temperatures, and they tend to warp in hot water.

THE COST OF ELECTRICITY

The amount of electricity a freezer uses depends on many factors other than the size of the model. Most of these other factors are under the control of the user and together critically determine the cost of operating the freezer. Money saved on food can easily be lost in unneccessarily high electricity costs due to poor freezer management.

The main factors affecting electricity consumption are:–

(a) *The efficiency of insulation in the walls of the cabinet.* This is the only non-management factor mentioned. The only way to ensure good insulation is to buy a reputable make recommended by a dealer or refrigeration engineer that you trust. Smaller freezers, having a greater surface area relative to internal capacity than larger freezers, are more expensive to keep cool. This does not contradict the earlier statement that food in a partially filled large freezer costs more per pound to keep cool than in a full small freezer. The critical factor is the packing density.

(b) *Packing density* will significantly affect electricity costs. Air is a poor conductor. The more air spaces in the freezer, whether around packages of food, between lids and food in plastic containers, or between layers or pieces of food, etc, the higher the electricity costs. Although a large freezer is an attractive proposition in terms of cubic capacity when purchased, if nearly empty for significant periods its running costs are high per pound of food. Using two smaller freezers, one which is in regular use whilst the other copes with garden produce in season and periods of cheap bulk meat but is switched off when empty, is a system of freezer management which has much to commend it, both in terms of operating costs and in avoiding some of the quality loss which follows from raising the temperature of already frozen food by freezing down food in the same freezer.

(c) *How much food you buy already frozen and how much you freeze down.* The home freezing of garden produce or large quantities of meat will mean that the freezer is running at maximum power consumption for long periods. This will put up electricity costs significantly.

(d) *Length of storage.* The longer food is kept in a freezer the greater the total electricity consumption per pound of food by the time it is eaten. Three to four months is the maximum *economic* time to keep the generally used frozen foods. In other words, aim at replacing the food in your freezer three to four times a year. The domestic freezer operating at −18°C is not keeping food as stable as the commercial cold store operating at −30°C, and so, for reasons of food quality loss as well as home freezer economics, aim at regular turnover of food in the freezer.

(e) *How frequently the door or lid of the freezer is opened and where the freezer is sited.* These two factors are grouped together because with modern well-designed equipment with efficient insulation, they are not very critical in the way they affect electricity consumption, compared with other factors mentioned. Of course, a freezer should not be sited in a warm place if a cool one is available, nor should the door or lid be opened more than is necessary. The design of many modern upright freezers minimizes any tendency for the upright freezer to lose cold air when the door is opened, compared with the loss from raising the lid of a chest freezer.

With the factors discussed in mind, can figures be put to electricity costs?

Table 1 shows the average electricity consumption of well managed freezers of different sizes, together with costs.

TABLE 1

Electricity consumption and costs

Size in cubic ft (and litres)	Electricity consumption (units per week)	Costs per week		Cost £ per year
		1p per unit	2·36p per unit*	
2(57)	2·5	2·5p	5·9p	3·06
4(113)	4·8	4·8p	11·3p	5·87
6(170)	6·6	6·6p	15·6p	8·10
8(227)	9·2	9·2p	21·7p	11·28
10(283)	10·0	10·0p	23·6p	12·27
12(340)	10·8	10·8p	25·5p	13·25
14(396)	11·9	11·9p	28·1p	14·60
16(453)	12·8	12·8p	30·2p	15·70
18(510)	13·5	13·5p	32·0p	16·56
20(566)	14·0	14·0p	33·0p	17·18

*2·36p per unit is an average price in 1977, costs for 1p per unit are given to help with calculations made as electricity prices increase.

If the packaging density is reduced by 50% eg from 20 lb food per cu. ft. to 10 lb per cu. ft., the operating costs go up as follows:—

For a 4 cu. ft. freezer by 80%; for a 10 cu. ft. freezer by 85%, and for a 20 cu. ft. freezer by 100%.

If food is kept in an under utilized freezer for a long period, the cost per pound to keep it is very high.

Figures of the order of 30p to keep a pound of food in an under utilized freezer for a year have been calculated, and although they do not reflect general home freezing operating costs, they stress the need for good freezer management to keep costs reasonable.

Minimizing freezer costs depends on:
1. Before buying the freezer consider carefully how you are going to use it. There is plenty of experience about, mainly from friends who have a freezer, to guide you.
2. Buy a freezer that is of the type and size for your considered needs.
3. Plan the stocking and turnover of food in the freezer.
4. Pack as densely as is possible without damaging food or making access difficult.
5. Buy food and packaging in bulk to gain maximum discount; batch bake and generally use the bulk store facility of the home freezer, to optimize all the kitchen practices that can be associated with home freezing, to help keep food costs down.

CHAPTER 3

Choosing a Freezer

THE PURCHASE of a freezer involves a considerable cash outlay, but once it has been acquired it is likely to be in use for many years. It is therefore important to be sure of the reliability of the freezer chosen and its suitability for family requirements.

Refrigerators have been designed from the earliest days to have a main compartment temperature suitable to extend storage life of food for a relatively short period. Early models had an "ice box", a small compartment which was cold enough to produce ice cubes. With the increasing appreciation of this colder section, particularly for holding commercially-frozen foods for a short period, the frozen food compartment has developed and now stretches across the top of the main compartment. To give a clear indication of the length of storage offered by the frozen food compartment the Star marking system has become well known:—

TABLE 2

	Compartment temperature	Storage time for frozen food
✼	−6°C (21°F)	up to 1 week
✼✼	−12°C (10°F)	up to 1 month
✼✼✼	−18°C (0°F)	up to 3 months

A refrigerator does not usually have the capacity to freeze food effciently and certainly not in anything more than very small quantities. A specialist freezer has this capacity and nowadays has its own symbol. The symbol shows the three stars preceded by a large white one (as below)

and this indicates power to hold food at −18°C or below and at the same time to freeze a certain proportion of its total capacity within 24 hours. Not every freezer has this symbol but it is an added assurance when present.

Although refrigerators are almost invariably designed with a front opening like a cupboard, freezers were originally developed as boxes or *chests* with a lid on top. This is probably because they evolved from ice cream conservators in which much early home freezing was done. However, conservators were only required to maintain the good quality of already-frozen ice cream and did not need to have the power to freeze food well. More recently, the *upright* or cabinet freezer has become equally popular, and there is a good choice of both types, from 60 litres (2 cu.ft.) to 700 litres (25 cu.ft.) upwards.

The *chest* type has a hinged lid on top which is usually counterbalanced to hold its position when open. Cold air is heavier than warm air so when the lid is opened there is very little loss of cold. This in turn prevents excessive frost formation and gives economical use of current. On the other hand, there is need for considerable bending and stretching in some cabinets to reach packages on the floor of the freezer, although this disadvantage can largely be overcome by storing frozen packs in baskets, bags or cartons which can be removed without too much exertion. The freezing of food is carried out in the coldest part of the freezer—usually in a small compartment over the motor (compressor). One drawback of this type of freezer is that the floor space required may be more than is available in the home.

The *upright* freezer with its front opening door gives good visibility of the contents and takes up little floor space. Cold air tends to fall out rapidly when the door is open. Warm air from the room is drawn in to replace it, and this air as it cools deposits its moisture in the form of frost which builds up round the door. Therefore, the advantage of good visibility in this type of freezer can have disadvantages. These can be minimized if the door is opened quickly to remove the food required and then closed without delay.

In an upright freezer the interior is divided by shelves, some of which may be removable, but most of which are fixed, with coils of refrigerant running through them. Thus, freezing of food can be carried out on any refrigerated shelf. A shield or baffle is arranged in some models in front of each shelf to reduce loss of cold and this can be effective provided it does not become immovable with ice. Baskets suspended from runners may replace some of the shelves: this arrangement makes the addition or removal of packets of food easier. Although the space between shelves is usually ample there may be occasions when it is difficult to fit in bulky or awkward-shaped packs.

The gasket forming the door seal may contain a low-powered heating circuit to prevent the build up of frost which could make the opening of the door an almost impossible task. Another refinement is a magnetic door closure which is more sure in use than a latch.

A newer design of upright freezer is *fan assisted*. The refrigerating unit is on top of the cabinet and the cooled air is circulated by a fan in the ceiling of the cabinet. Automatic defrosting is a feature of this type of freezer. Air is heated for a short period every twenty-four hours and this thaws any frost that has been formed in the cabinet. It drips into a collecting tray where it refreezes and can be removed about once a fortnight. The freezing performance of this design is good. The overall cost is about 25% more than for a conventional upright freezer of the same capacity.

Another alternative is the *combined refrigerator-freezer*. There are many on the market but the freezer capacity is usually small. Ideally the freezer should be as large if not larger than the refrigerator but it is difficult, if not impossible, to achieve the two different temperatures required unless there are dual refrigeration units which increase the price considerably.

Investigation behind one of the dearer types will usually reveal two compressors which indicates that good performance should be obtained. Where one unit is used, there may be difficulty in attaining correct freezer temperature without wilting of vegetables and freezing of milk in the refrigerator because it is too cold.

The refrigeration system is basically the same for chest and upright models. The liquid refrigerant circulates through the *evaporator tubes* which lie just below the surface of the inner casing. The food freezing compartment should be well provided with these tubes. In upright freezers the tubes are visible under shelves but in chest types their presence may be indicated by rounded ridges in the casing. The secure and close fixing of these tubes to the casing helps to ensure efficient and economical performance on a long-term basis.

Heat from the food vaporises the refrigerant which is re-cooled by circulation through the *compressor* to the *condenser* and then recirculates. The main task of the refrigerating unit is to freeze food and maintain it at a temperature of $-18°C$ ($0°F$), but a considerable amount of energy is required to remove the heat that, even with good insulation, leaks into the chest. This will be in the region of 13 units per week for a 280 litre (10 cu. ft.)* chest freezer, and more when the freezer is housed in a warm room and when the freezer door is opened frequently or for too long.

The rating or electrical power of the compressor should be ascertained. If, for example, one 420 litre (15 cu. ft.) freezer has a $\frac{1}{4}$ hp compressor and another has a $\frac{1}{3}$ hp compressor, the latter should give faster freezing and therefore a better quality product. While it is running it will consume more current and may initially be a little dearer to purchase, but the extra expense is well justified.

Condensers have three forms. First, on small capacity upright freezers, the condensing coil may form a grid on the back of the model. This is the usual cooling method for domestic refrigerators, and for satisfactory performance a good 5 cm (2″) clearance is necessary to allow for air circulation. Secondly, in chest freezers, the condensing tubes may be attached immediately beneath the outer casing. The presence of these tubes can be checked by feeling the warmth on one's hand from the side of a freezer in use. This system is known as a *skin condenser* and it has the advantage of minimising condensation on the surface of

*1 cubic foot = 28 litres

the freezer but it loses efficiency in high ambient temperatures. Thirdly, a *fan-assisted* condenser may be used on chest or upright models and is efficient if somewhat more costly. The condenser, housed near the compressor, is cooled by a fan which draws air through vents at floor level. The vents are usually covered with a grille and the grilles and the fan blades must be kept free of fluff and dust, but usually twice-yearly cleaning will be sufficient. The vents need air space which must be allowed when siting the freezer.

THERMOMETER

Several references have been made to temperature. The selected thermostat setting should give an air temperature maximum of $-18°C$ (0°F) in the freezer, which can be checked by using a freezer thermometer. One would expect this to be a standard fitting but unfortunately it is not and freezer owners are advised to buy a thermometer, the cost of which is about £1·50.

ASSESSING FAMILY REQUIREMENTS
CAPACITY AND SITING

These two considerations must be dovetailed. It is probably best to consider the ideal capacity first and then the site. In this way a previously unconsidered site may be discovered or contrived whereas by deciding the site first, capacity may be more limited than necessary.

It is advisable to forecast approximately the amount of food the freezer will be required to hold, such as:

    (i) own produce—garden or farm

    (ii) bulk purchasing—
        kind of food
        whether frozen or fresh

    (iii) own cookery
        prepared meals
        baked goods

    (iv) other items e.g. catering for special occasions

It was formerly considered that commercially up to 500 g per litre (30 lb. per cu. ft.) was a possible loading density, given uniform packs of good weight. However, for home use, it is more realistic to reckon about 300/340 g per litre (18/20 lb. per cu. ft.). Thus, a 140 litre (5 cu. ft.) freezer might in use hold 42/56 kg (90/100 lb.) which could be made up as follows:

TABLE 3

Food	Metric		Imperial	
	Volume litres	Weight kg	Volume cu. ft.	Weight lb
Boneless meat and poultry	56	25	2	55
Fruit and vegetables	42	14	$1\frac{1}{2}$	30
Made up dishes, gâteaux, etc.	42	7	$1\frac{1}{2}$	15
	140	46	5	100

It will be seen from the foregoing example that the packing density of the different foods varies. Boneless meat will pack at over 500 g per litre but the inclusion of some carcase poultry lowers the overall density for that section. Delicate desserts and gâteaux require protective wrapping and they are extravagant with freezer space. It is not necessary, or, in fact possible, to attempt a complete forecast of the freezer's use but a rough assessment will indicate the size required.

Another approach is to consider the volume of food per head which will be frozen, and 110 litres (4 cu.ft.) per person is suggested if fairly substantial use is to be made of frozen foods. For a household of 6 people this might prove more than adequate, whereas for one it could be too little.

As a second freezer, a very small model may be chosen to stand in the kitchen to supplement a larger model elsewhere, but there are very few occasions when a small freezer (under 75 litres i.e. 3 cu. ft.) is a good initial purchase.

A good rate of turnover, as shown in Chapter 2, gives a more economical use of the freezer.

Where large quantities of home-killed or other unfrozen meat are available, the maximum quantity that can be frozen in one day will be important, (see page 22), and the purchase of a larger freezer may be worthwhile. Alternatively it may be more economical to arrange for the meat to be frozen at the abattoir or by the butcher and then brought home. Similarly when autumn-culled poultry is held frozen for a few weeks to obtain the better Christmas prices, commercial freezing rates may be more economical than buying extra freezing space for short term use.

There are many considerations to meet family requirements but a common complaint is that the first freezer purchased is soon found to be too small to take advantage of all it offers.

SITING

It must be borne in mind that a loaded freezer is heavy and therefore needs a strong floor. Most freezers are made to pass through a standard doorway but it requires considerable skill to negotiate a large freezer through a small space. A right-angled turn in a narrow passage may prove impossible. Some freezer doors open within the width of the cabinet. Others need extra space for which allowance must be made. With chest types, the lid must be free to open fully without hitting shelves or wall cupboards. Some air space should be allowed all round a freezer, depending on the type of condenser. If the freezer stands on feet or on runners they must not be removed as air space underneath is necessary.

A refrigerator is needed for frequent use and is obviously required in the kitchen. A freezer can more economically be kept in a cooler place provided it is dry and the temperature is not likely to drop below 4°C (40°F) in cold weather. If the freezer is to be kept away from the home, in a garage or outbuilding, it is wise to buy a model with a lock. Damp, unventilated outbuildings should be avoided because in such situations rust is inevitable. It attacks the metal parts underneath the freezer and is often unobserved until too late. The freezer should stand on a wooden platform to avoid contact with a damp floor. Freezers function satisfactorily in warm kitchens but for economy they should be kept away from the cooker, the boiler and sunny windows and skylights.

THE FINAL CHOICE

While considering the site for a freezer, the question of whether to go for a chest or an upright will probably have settled itself, but it is still advisable to see as many models as possible of the type required, or of both types if the choice is open. This is not always easy as most suppliers only carry a few models of two or three makes, but freezer-owning friends can be helpful at this stage, especially in sharing their experiences. A good range can usually be seen at appropriate Exhibitions. When looking at freezers, the *temperature control panel* should be studied. It is usually sited low down on the freezer, but there is no rule for this. The panel generally has one light that stays on all the time the freezer is connected, so that should the light be out you know that the freezer has been switched off or that there is an interruption of the electricity supply. It gives no indication of temperature in the freezer but it indicates a fault by the absence of its light. Some freezers have a second light which (a) is only on when the freezer temperature is within the safety range or, (b) is only on when the freezer is too warm. This second type is less useful than the first, as in current failure it would not be functioning. Thirdly, on this panel, there is a switch and a light. This is the *Super-Freeze* or *Fast Freeze* which, when switched on, cuts out the normal cycling of the motor to give continuous running until it is switched off. Continuous running gives the lowest temperature the motor can achieve and this switch is used to speed the freezing rate when fresh food is put in. Its use is described in Chapter 4. Finally, there will probably be a dial with a range of numbers, say, 1 to 6. This sets the thermostat to ensure correct temperature within the freezer.

While looking at the exterior, the material, quality, sturdiness and finish of the case can be evaluated and the type of condenser noted. The outer casing is usually of enamelled metal, but it could be plastic or, in expensive models, stainless steel. It should not be liable to dent or fracture and it should be able to withstand delivery hazards as well as normal use. The freezer may be mounted on castors and this is an advantage—or a hazard with high-spirited children!

Opening the freezer gives an opportunity to examine the door or lid construction, the latch or magnetic seal, and the gasket (door seal) which must be resilient and fit tightly. Chest freezer lids are counter-balanced to hold them open and should be tested for opening rigidly, without any tendency to waver. This will indicate good cross-bracing which is essential for such a large area. Insulation is most important. The modern method of using foamed polyurethane pumped between the outer and inner moulded shells gives good performance combined with space-saving. Hence the modern freezer may appear under-insulated in comparison with early models. The interior casing is usually vitreous or stove-enamelled steel, but it may be metal-lined or plastic. Doors or lids are usually plastic-lined. In the lid and the body there should be no suspicion of weakness at joins as the preservation of the insulation is essential.

The presence of a freezing compartment in a chest freezer must be checked. Not all freezers have them. In an upright, the shelves should be inspected. Are some removable? Are there evaporating tubes under all those that are fixed? Is there sufficient space available for, say, a turkey? The appeal of the fittings is an individual matter. They should be easy to manipulate, strong and have real purpose. The depth of large chest freezers should be tested by the shortest person who has to use it. The delving can be improved with baskets or large bags to collect foods of a kind together but deep chests are for the active.

If the freezer does not carry the Freezer Symbol, a written guarantee should be available stating that its performance is to symbol standards. There should be an instruction book and also an official statement of the nett capacity, the motor rating and arrangements for servicing and, perhaps, for insurance.

Local servicing agents are important as in a breakdown speedy attention is essential. Insurance of contents may be offered at the time of purchase. Premiums are moderate compared with the present-day value of a freezer load of food. Freezer insurance can, on the other hand, usually be added at small charge to an existing household insurance.

Despite careful examination, the purchaser will not necessarily be able to check all aspects. Great care should be exercised before deciding to purchase any model that is significantly cheaper than others of the same type and size, particularly regarding motor power, nett capacity, refrigerating unit and general construction. To conclude, most freezer manufacturers produce sound long-lasting products and the great majority of freezer owners are well satisfied with their equipment.

CHAPTER 4

The Care and Use of a Freezer

BEFORE USE

WHEN THE freezer is installed, and before it is switched on, it is advisable to wash it out with water containing a level dessertspoonful of bicarbonate of soda per quart. Detergents should not be used because of their added perfume. The interior should be rinsed, well dried and the current then switched on. If there is a choice of settings on the dial, it is advisable to use a middle position. A freezer thermometer (Chapter 3, p. 17) is essential to ascertain the correct dial setting. After three or four hours the thermometer reading should be taken and the setting adjusted to give a temperature of $-18°$ to $-20°C$ ($0°$ to $-4°F$) in the centre of the cabinet.

The thermometer should then be placed in various other positions in the freezer, especially in large upright models, and the dial setting adjusted to ensure that the recommended maximum temperature is not exceeded in any area. The lower the temperature, the better the quality retention of frozen food, but the temperatures given above ensure a balance between quality and economical running costs.

TO FREEZE FOOD

As considerable heat has to be removed from food to take it from the unfrozen to the frozen state (p. 4, Ch. 1), it is necessary to lower the temperature of the food already in the freezer as much as possible before adding further food and to observe the load limit. Where a fast or super freeze switch is available, this should be switched on before food is put in. For a maximum load it is best to switch to fast freeze an hour or two in advance. Similarly, where there is no fast freeze switch the dial setting should be turned to the lowest position. Prepared food should be frozen without delay, but if refrigerator space is available it is best to use it to cool the packs for an hour or two before placing them in the freezer. The preliminary cooling in the refrigerator takes out heat that would otherwise use up some of the freezer's reserve of cold.

Not more than 30 g of food per litre (2 lb. per cu. ft.) of freezer capacity should be frozen per 24 hours, e.g., in a 280 litre (10 cu. ft.) freezer a load of 9 kg (20 lb.) should be the maximum at one time. The packs should be spread out in the freezing section, if provided, and in any case, in contact with the walls or shelves housing the evaporator tubes. Where bulk quantities of unfrozen meat are purchased, this limitation on weight may pose a problem.

The food is usually left in the freezing compartment until the next day, although a small load, put into the freezer in the morning, will be frozen within six to ten hours and can be moved for more food to be frozen.

When freezing is complete, the fast freezing switch should be turned off or the dial returned to its normal setting. For a full freezing load the fast freeze switch should be left on for 20–24 hours, for a half load 10–12 hours, etc.

STORAGE OF FROZEN FOOD

Even with a small freezer it is necessary to have a storage plan. With chest-type freezers, one or two baskets may be supplied as part of the equipment. These usually slide along the top of the chest and the lower part is an open space with possibly one or two dividers. Spare baskets can be purchased. When measuring dimensions for baskets, a small allowance for manipulation should be made. Although this latitude loses a little storage space, it permits easy removal and re-arrangement of baskets. If cheaper containers are required, large polyethylene bags or the modern nylon equivalent of the string bag will be found useful.

When the food is frozen, packs of the same kind should be gathered together and stored in a particular container or part of the freezer. If commercially frozen food is purchased, it should be put immediately into its storage position. The upright cabinet gives easier visibility of contents but even so it is not possible to see to the back of a well-stocked shelf and so a storage plan is necessary. Coloured wraps, labels or even marking crayon are necessary for quick identification. Stress is laid upon speed as the freezer should be opened for as short a period as possible to prevent loss of cold and build up of frost. This is particularly important with front-opening types.

RECORD KEEPING

In conjunction with the freezer, it is essential to have a record of stocks of frozen food. A few people enjoy elaborate recording but it is probably fair to say that for the majority it is a necessary but often neglected chore. It is therefore best to use as simple a method as possible and one that appeals to the individual user. A simple book or card index can be purchased for keeping such a record, but a small note book with ring binding is sufficient in most homes. Where foods are seasonal there is no need to note the date when frozen, but keen gardeners may wish to record cultivar, date of sowing, harvesting, weight of waste, etc. It may be found simplest to give quantities in terms of portions although some prefer to put actual weights. It is advisable to enter packs individually so that they can be struck off as used, e.g.

BROCCOLI— portions ~~2~~ ~~2~~ ~~2~~ ~~4~~ 4 6 4 4 2 2 2

For food with a limited recommended storage period, note must be made of the date when frozen, or preferably, the date by which it should be eaten.

The value of a record for keeping a tally on stocks is obvious. It will also be more reliable than memory in indicating which foods have been most popular and should be increased in quantity in the coming season and, conversely, those that can be reduced.

REMOVAL OF FROZEN FOOD

The time of removal of food from the freezer will depend on its thawing rate or further treatment before serving, and it can vary from over two days before use for a large frozen turkey, to the point of use for frozen vegetables, boil-in-the-bag meals or small portions of meat or fish.

Before opening the freezer, the operator should remind himself/herself where the required food is stored so that the door is only open long enough for the pack to be removed and the remaining stock tidied up if necessary. It is worthwhile cultivating the habit of thought before opening the freezer as, over a period of time, the build-up of frost will be less if door opening periods are kept short. When the food is eaten it is important to cross off the appropriate entry in the record book, which is best kept, with pencil attached, near the freezer.

DEFROSTING

There is an inevitable build-up of frost round the opening of a freezer. With a chest-type freezer, the air in the chest is relatively undisturbed, as cold air is heavier than air at room temperature. However, some warmer air is bound to be introduced when a package is put in or removed, and a small interchange of warm and cold air takes place at the top level of the freezer. With upright models, there is much more 'fall out' of cold air and consequently more room air is drawn in. As the temperature of the air drops, it inevitably deposits its moisture in the form of frost. The interchange of air normally takes place around the opening and this is where the frost builds up. Unfortunately, some people still connect the presence of a thick layer of frost with good refrigeration, whereas in fact it is a barrier to efficient cooling. Frost should be removed as soon as it is about 1 cm ($\frac{1}{2}$ inch) thick, and this can be easily done with a wooden or plastic scraper. Such a scraper is in many cases a part of the equipment supplied with the freezer, but a wooden spatula or ruler can be used. Knives and other metal blades are not suitable as they can easily damage the lining of the freezer. As the scraping takes place, the loosened frost can be caught on a tray and thrown away—unless required as distilled water for, say, use in a steaming iron. The regular removal of frost may seem a negative task, but frost not removed soon consolidates into ice which is much more difficult to clear.

CLEANING THE FREEZER

If frost is removed weekly or fortnightly, there will be little build-up of ice and annual defrosting will be sufficient for chest freezers. Front-opening types will probably need defrosting two or three times a year but this depends on the efficiency of use and the ambient temperature. With frequent opening in a warm kitchen, upright freezers will require more defrosting than a chest in similar conditions.

If possible it is best to defrost when stocks are low because less effort is required, but the magnitude of the task is not as great as many expect. Switch off the current, remove and stack all the contents compactly on layers of newspaper in a cool situation and cover with a rug or blanket or more newspapers. Take out any loose fittings from the freezer and put a tray or trays and a folded towel in the bottom. Stand one or two bowls of hot water in the freezer and close the lid. Open up in 10 to 15 minutes and, if any ice is loosening, remove it in a piece. If it is still firm, replenish the water, close the lid or door and wait a further quarter of an hour before trying again. This demands a little time but a great deal of mopping up can be avoided if the bulk of the ice is removed before it thaws. More drastic treatments with hair dryers or fan heaters are not recommended because the freezer lining may be damaged. Once all the ice has been taken away, remove the towel and trays which should hold most of the drip, but it is usually necessary to have a final mop round inside. If there are any stains or odour. a wash with water containing 1 level dessertspoonful of bicarbonate of soda per quart should be effective but if not, try 4 tablespoonfuls of vinegar per quart. After using either of these, rinse with clear water and thoroughly dry the interior if still wet.

Replace the cleaned fittings, switch on the freezer and replace the food. This whole operation can be completed in an hour or less with a small freezer. The sooner the frozen food is back in the freezer the better but, at the same time, handling the frozen packs gives the opportunity to check them with the record and this is well worth doing. Common faults are forgetting to cross food off the record when it is eaten and putting in odd items without listing them. Defrosting time gives a chance to get the record straight and to bring forward any packs that have been overlooked.

The exterior of the cabinet will benefit from cleaning and the manufacturer's instructions should be followed. The top of a chest freezer offers an expanse on which a variety of utensils will inevitably be placed temporarily. To protect the surface a sheet of polyethylene secured to the edge of the lid with a sealing tape is effective and replaceable when necessary at small cost.

DEALING WITH AN EMERGENCY

Under this heading are grouped together the mechanical, electrical or human faults that could lead to loss of function in the freezer.

Although this situation is one that is feared by potential freezer owners, it is rarely experienced at a serious level and, even then, in many cases damage to food can be minimised by knowledge of correct procedure.

For initial reassurance, the results of tests show that provided the freezer is reasonably well filled and the door is kept closed, many hours will elapse after breakdown before a thawing temperature is reached. With a 110 litre (4 cu.ft.) front-opening freezer, half filled, a period of over eight hours was required for the warmest peak to reach −5°C (23°F), at which temperature most foods are not thawing. Similarly, food in fully-loaded 8 and 12 cubic feet top-opening freezers showed no visible signs of thawing for nearly 12 hours and over 17 hours, respectively. These examples are both from relatively small freezers and the food in a well packed large freezer of say, 560 litres (20 cu. ft.) capacity, should survive a much longer interruption without safety risk or undue quality loss. It must be stressed that good cold-retention can only be expected in freezers packed to a density of over 300 g per litre (18lb. per cu.ft.) and not subject to door opening.

In emergency situations, the value of a warning device is apparent as otherwise the failure may be unobserved for a considerable time. The most common fault is the accidental switching off of either the freezer switch or the main switch. A strip of sealing tape over the freezer switch will prevent absent-minded accidents. The main switch is more vital as the damage is likely to be severe if the house is to be left empty for several days. It is not always easy to fix a notice to a main switch but some device can usually be contrived to remind the departing householder. Many people are loth to leave the main supply on during holidays and some authorities allow special wiring to the freezer.

If the freezer is not functioning:

1. Check that the freezer switch is on.
2. Test the general supply to the house first to ascertain the extent of the fault. If there is no supply, check with neighbours whether the fault is general and if so wait a couple of hours before telephoning the Electricity Board for information about the expected duration. Many faults are corrected within two hours.
3. If the fault is confined to the supply to one's own house, telephone the Electricity Board at once.
4. If supply is coming into the house, check other outlets on the same circuit as the freezer. If they are not functioning, turn off the main switch and replace the circuit fuse with an appropriate fuse, switch on the main, and test. If there is no general response, telephone the electrician.
5. If there is no freezer response, switch off the freezer and check the lead and its connection to the plug, change the fuse in the plug, switch on and test.
6. If there is no response, telephone the service engineers.

Remember that the food will be safe in the freezer for several hours and restrain the impulse to look inside. It is sometimes recommended that a blanket should be placed over the freezer while it is out of action. This is of marginal benefit in most circumstances and unless removed as soon as supply is resumed could handicap the working of the freezer.

In the unlikely event of a really long delay, the freezer temperature can be maintained by the use of frozen carbon dioxide which may be obtainable from an ice-cream depot. Great care must be taken with this intensely cold material. Heavy gloves must be worn to handle it and it must not come into direct contact with plastic surfaces or polyethylene wraps as they could be damaged. One kilogram of carbon dioxide is sufficient to keep 8 kg (18 lb) of frozen food in good condition in the freezer for 2 to 3 days. The carbon dioxide (Cardice, Dri-Cold) should be left in large pieces, placed securely in a folded newspaper and put on the top layer of packages in the freezer. The cooled air will fall from the refrigerant down through the freezer and there is no need to re-arrange the packaging apart from making room at the top. Those living in rural areas where prolonged breakdowns are a possibility are well advised to find out in advance where supplies can be obtained.

In the case of a major freezer breakdown without the possibility of immediate replacement, the food can be packed into cartons and stored in a Cold Storage depot where the charge made will be based on the weight or the volume and the period of storage. The need for this is a remote possibility but it is useful to know in advance where such help can be found. When using commercial cold storage it is advisable to stress the temperature of the storage required.

CONDITION OF THAWED FOOD

When the freezer is found to be off and the duration of the failure is unknown, the condition of the food rightly causes concern. Foods that are quickly perishable in unfrozen use, e.g., made-up dishes, shell fish, are similarly quickly perishable when thawed. If the package when pressed in the hand 'crunches' to indicate the presence of ice crystals, it can be re-frozen and used as soon as possible. The re-freezing will detract from its quality but it will be safe. With fully thawed food the safest course is to destroy it. With absolutely sweet-smelling fruit or fruit products, they can be prepared in a cooked dish and eaten, or cooled and frozen, for consumption as soon as possible. Ice cream cannot be re-frozen and remain an acceptable product because the normal texture is lost.

A loaded freezer that has been off for a week or more presents a depressing sight. The food must be burnt or carefully buried. The freezer will need several thorough washings and should be left open for a long period under cover, in fresh air. The use of strong-smelling detergents is normally avoided in freezers but in this situation they may be necessary to banish the bad smell.

Faults of this magnitude are, unfortunately, frequently due to human error, and it is therefore worth repeating the advisability of 'sealing' the switch in the 'On' position with a strip of adhesive tape and putting a warning label on the main switch.

An insurance will not cover human error but the cost of the contents can be recovered in the case of mechanical breakdown.

CHAPTER 5

Choice and Use of Packaging

FOOD FREEZING allows a wide choice of packaging materials, from the relatively flimsy polyethylene bag to the rigid, self-sealing container and sophisticated laminates. The basic requirements that must be met are:

1. SAFETY

The material itself must be non-toxic and it must be clean. New purpose-made wraps stored hygienically present no risk. If re-used, wraps need careful washing, drying and storage as food fragments not removed could become a health hazard. Polyethylene bags are perhaps the most difficult to keep clean for re-use and, as they are inexpensive, they are best used only once.

The use of rigid packs which originally contained some other food, e.g., margarine, yogurt, is unlikely to present any hazard, but containers made for non-foods should be avoided.

2. FOOD QUALITY RETENTION

The material must be:

(a) Moisture/vapour-proof to prevent: (i) dehydration of the contents, (ii) oxidation, and consequent loss of colour and nutrients, (iii) transfer of flavour from one pack to another, (iv) leakage.

(b) Protective: (i) to shield tender foods, e.g., gâteaux, from physical damage, and (ii) to prevent uneven packs from piercing the wrap, e.g., protruding bones on joints.

(c) Non-odorous to avoid flavouring contents.

(d) Not brittle at freezer temperatures, to avoid breakage and spoilage of contents.

3. EASE IN USE

Ease in wrapping prevents delay in getting the prepared food into the freezer. The pack required depends on the nature of the food and time can be lost with a too slippery or too stubborn material that might be ideal in a different connection. The ease of sealing, labelling, stacking, and finally of unwrapping should all be considered.

4. ECONOMIC COST

The cheapest home wrap is a bulk purchase (1000 or more) of 120 or 150-gauge polyethylene bags. When only used once they are still good value for general purposes, although they may require an overwrap for uneven packs. It is economical to standardize on one or two sizes and order these in quantity rather than to buy several sizes in small numbers. However, if much of the freezer space is used for delicate dishes, a considerable outlay on good quality rigid containers that could be used repeatedly may be justified. Initially, many types are tried but it is economically advisable to limit the range as soon as possible in order to buy a few types at bulk prices.

TYPES OF PACKAGING MATERIAL FOR FROZEN FOODS

Before considering purpose-made materials, it must be remembered that water is often used to 'wrap' or glaze fish. In the home, fish, whole or in portions, can be frozen and then dipped in ice-cold water. It is then returned to the freezer and the treatment repeated until a clinging glaze of ice completely covers and protects the fish. An overwrap of polyethylene prevents the ice from chipping.

POLYETHYLENE. This adaptable material has much to recommend it as a wrap for packs not requiring rigidity. The minimum gauge recommended is 120 and at this strength should be regarded as expendable after initial use. It may be considered that the slight extra cost of 150-gauge is repaid by extra strength, and for repeated use for heavier, larger packs, 250-guage can be obtained to order. However, it is more difficult to make a tight fitting pack with the 250-guage. Polyethylene is available in sheet, bag or tube form, and the range of sizes is almost unlimited. A 'box' or gussetted bag or tube gives a square pack and stacks more economically than its ungussetted counterpart. Brightly coloured polyethylene bags can be obtained and these are useful for quick recognition of contents. In use, a polyethylene bag filled with soft food, such as sauce, will freeze into a space-wasting oval shape, and it is useful to keep a few cartons into which such packs can be placed until they are frozen. This will ensure a rectangular shape that will pack economically. As these cartons will only have to be in the freezer for up to 12 hours, any clean, reasonably strong food container can be used, e.g., dried fruit or caster sugar packets. Polyethylene bags with an aluminium foil or paper outer casing are available to give extra protection or, alternatively, a home-made foil wrap can be used. Double-wrapping slows down the rate of freezing if there is air entrapped between the layers.

It is easier to expel the air and to seal the bag when there is room to spare than with a close fit, so small bags should be avoided. Polyethylene bags take up little room and, provided they are kept covered, dry and away from odours and mice, they will store for years.

CELLULOSE TISSUE. The use of this material for frozen foods has been developed more commercially than domestically. It is important to use the correct moisture and vapour-proof grade for freezing which is MSAT 300/30. It has the advantage of easy heat-sealing (see p. 34) but is more difficult to handle then polyethylene.

BOIL-IN-THE-BAG. These bags, originally produced to withstand immersion in boiling water, have in many cases been found suitable for use in the freezer. This has the advantage that prepared foods can be packed, frozen and finally re-heated in the same bag, without even dirtying a saucepan. The size of the bag usually limits the contents to single portions which is convenient for serving. Larger packs are not satisfactory for most foods as the re-heating period is too long. Several bags can be heated together in the same saucepan of boiling water, e.g., a bag of rice, a bag of chicken curry and a bag of stewed fruit. Some salad and chutney would complete the first course and a little cream the second. Care is essential in sealing these bags. Suitable ties are provided by some suppliers and very reliable electric heat sealers are available if home use is sufficient to justify the outlay of a few pounds. .

ALUMINIUM FOIL. The usual household grade is scarcely strong enough to withstand the inevitable friction of one pack against another in the freezer. It is, however, very useful for buffering projecting bone ends. The heavy duty grade (0·025 mm) is suitable for wrapping and it has sufficient rigidity to give some support to the contents. A strip of foil can be folded in half and joined up the sides with a double fold to enclose a food which, after freezing, can be boiled in the foil bag. Foil dishes are very convenient for prepared meals and cooked dishes in the freezer as they can be taken from freezer to oven to table. Heavy-duty foil can be used to make additional lids for these containers. If acid foods such as fruit are being used, the foil should be one with a suitable acid resistant lacquer. This lacquer may be colourless, so it is not possible to determine its presence by sight.

SPECIALLY PREPARED PAPERS. Various papers are available in rolls for food freezing and may be preferred to foil for some baked products. Untreated paper would be unsuitable because it lacks moisture-vapour-proof qualities.

RIGID CONTAINERS. These are most commonly made of plastic or foil. Glass is not recommended because of its fragility during freezing and thawing, and its bulk. Waxed cartons are cheaper than plastic, but have a shorter life and, to avoid staining, lining with a polyethylene bag is recommended. Foil containers may have rather poor fitting lids, but many types of plastic container have really close fitting covers. The initial cost is comparatively high, but they are very long wearing. Soft fruits repay freezing in rigid containers. An increasing number of foods are sold in plastic containers and these can be cleaned and used in the freezer. Although tubs often use freezer space wastefully, yogurt or cream cartons make very useful containers for small items such as egg whites or lemon juice. If a rigid container is too large for the portions required, it is usually possible to sub-divide it by foil or polyethylene strips. Baking tins can be put in the freezer but the housewife soon finds her supply depleted. The same situation exists with casseroles and cooking dishes and, additionally with these, to avoid cracking the dish, the food must be partially thawed before putting in the oven. The one exception at present is the type of dish made from a material which withstands the thermal shock of removal from −18°C (0°F) to +200°C (390°F) in the oven, for example, Pyrosil or Pyroflam.

UNDERWRAPS. When packing meat and poultry, projecting bone ends must be covered to prevent them puncturing the outer wrap, and greaseproof paper or foil is the usual choice. Similarly, with small cuts of meat such as chops or slices of liver, a double-fold of greaseproof paper must be placed between each piece and the next so that as many as are required can be removed. Without inter-leaving with double paper, the slices would freeze together in one piece.

OVERWRAPS. Large uneven packs are liable to tear, and therefore an overwrap of mutton cloth (circular knit stockinet) is advisable.

HEADSPACE

Water expands in the freezing process and, for some foods, allowance must be made for this expansion, otherwise the wrap will burst. Some foods, such as blanched vegetables, can be packed without allowing for expansion, but when packing a block of raw pastry or boned meat it is advisable to allow a small pleat in the wrap, to take up any expansion. Fruit packed plain should have about 2·5 cm (1 in) headspace per kg and for fruit in syrup, up to 5 cm (2 in) per kg. The air in the headspace above the syrup will cause browning of light fruits and therefore a rigid container is used, and a piece of clean crumpled greaseproof paper is placed over the fruit. The pressure of the lid on the paper keeps the fruit submerged and a good colour.

Colour will be lost very quickly from light fruits when trimmed, peeled and cored. It will be preserved if the measured syrup is placed in the container first and the fruit dropped in as soon as it is prepared.

PACKING AND SEALING

In all packing as much air as possible should be excluded to minimize oxidative changes. Where a flat sheet of wrap is used, there are two usual methods. The druggist's fold is recommended for fairly rectangular shapes. The food is placed square on an ample size sheet,

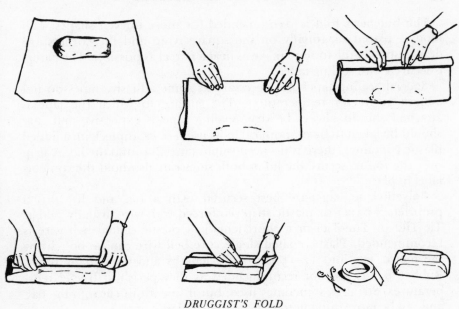

DRUGGIST'S FOLD

the wrap is drawn up close to the food on both sides and joined in a double-fold along the top of the food. The ends are similarly turned in with a double-fold and the whole secured with sealing tape.

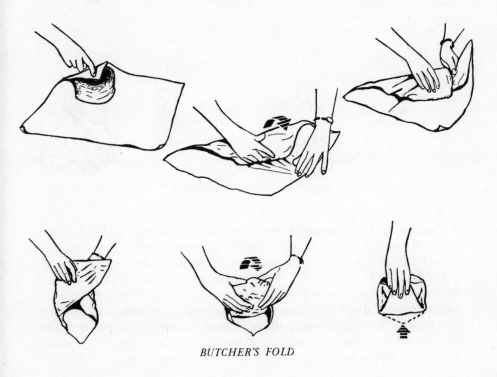

BUTCHER'S FOLD

The butcher's fold is recommended for more uneven shapes. The food is placed diagonally on the square wrap and the corners are drawn up over the food to make as neat a parcel as possible. The parcel is secured with sealing tape.

Special sealing tapes are necessary as some adhesive tapes do not adhere at freezer temperatures. The surface to which the tape is attached should always be dry. Sealing tape is expensive and care should be taken to be economical in its use. For example, with a lidded plastic container, there is no need to put tape all round the lid. A strip over the top to secure the lid at both sides can also hold the contents label in place.

Polyethylene bags are best secured with a tie, and for this a proprietary paper or plastic strip reinforced with wire (usually sold as Tie-Tite or Tite-Tie) or a short length of plastic-coated bell wire is recommended. Plastic-coated single core bell wire can be bought by the metre, cut into 12–15 cm (5–6″) lengths and used many times. Rubber bands are not recommended as they perish at freezer temperatures. String is sometimes used, but if fine it can cut into the bag and can be more difficult to remove than a plastic tie.

An important stage before sealing is to exclude as much air as possible from the pack. In this connection it will be found helpful when using a bag to have sufficient spare space to press out the air and to twist the neck of the bag tightly for about 5 cm (2 in). This twist is then turned back on itself and the tie is firmly secured over the double twist.

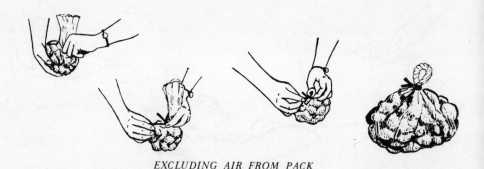

EXCLUDING AIR FROM PACK

Commercial heat sealing is much used in conjunction with a vacuum pack. Heat sealing can be undertaken at home using a warm electric iron, but it will be found difficult to exclude the air, although it may be possible to fold over the bag before sealing and thus prevent re-entry of air. The surfaces to be joined must be dry. With cellulose tissue heat can be applied direct to the surfaces to be joined, but with polyethylene it is necessary to insert a strip of tissue paper or other material between the heated iron and the packing material. For this purpose a special double strip can be bought. Special heat sealing irons are available, but if an electric iron is used it should be pre-heated on the nylon setting and used on its side so that its edge applies the heat. Care must be taken when using an iron on its side as it is liable to twist and burn the operator's arm. In fact, it has been found that few home freezer owners make a practice of heat sealing unless they have a special bag sealer. Where the cost of special apparatus is justified, this method has much to recommend it.

LABELLING

It is important to label packs of food before putting them in the freezer. As with record keeping, most people realize the necessity for labelling but find it rather a chore. It is advisable to evolve a plan that gives the required information without unnecessary detail. In addition to the name of the food itself, the quantity (weight or number of portions), date and any other details should be given. For example, the keen labeller might write:

12 oz strawberries

(Talisman)

in 3 oz caster sugar

27.6.77

whereas a busy housewife might well be satisfied with:

Strawberries in sugar for 3

June 77

Obviously, the more detail that is recorded, the more one can assess preferences.

The quickest method of labelling bags is to use the type of tie that has one end longer and broader to make a label. Details can be written on this and then the tie is used to seal the bag so that sealing and labelling are completed at the same time.

Stick-on labels in various sizes are now made specially to withstand freezer temperatures. As ink tends to smudge in the freezer, pencil, waxed crayon (chinagraph), or felt pen are recommended. Where polyethylene bags are being used once only, the details can be written direct on the bag, but it is advisable to use a colour that contrasts with the contents. It may be said that it is not necessary to label the bag at all, but it is not easy to tell one frozen vegetable from another at a glance and the use of a label makes it unnecessary to keep the freezer open while packets are examined. Additionally, the label gives information about portion size and date frozen; facts which could not be seen.

UTILIZATION

Experience will show which type of pack is most convenient to remove when the food is to be used. Long strips of adhesive tape wound round a container lid are unnecessary, wasteful and extremely frustrating to remove, but ties untwist easily. A self-sealing plastic container may need a little thawing under cold running water before the lid can be removed. Foil is best self-sealed by double-folds so that it can be opened out smoothly and washed for re-use.

Thin 120-gauge polyethylene bags are best discarded; other wraps should be washed in clean water with detergent, rinsed, drained and dried thoroughly. Leave in a warm kitchen overnight to ensure dryness before packing away in a clean place. Lidded containers should be stored open, not sealed.

Points for Successful Packaging:

1. Use moisture/vapour-proof wraps of a type and size suitable for the contents.
2. Economize by buying in bulk.
3. Re-use rigid food containers.
4. Pack to exclude the air but allow appropriate headspace before sealing securely.
5. Label clearly and record at once.
6. Discard thin-guage polyethylene bags after single use.
7. For re-use of packaging, wash and dry carefully before storing in a clean place free from taints or smells.

CHAPTER 6

Vegetables

VEGETABLES FOR freezing should be of a suitable variety and picked at their prime. With home grown crops there is often a tendency to enjoy the freshly cooked vegetable and to delay picking for freezing until peak condition has passed. Similarly, as the condition of the crop and the speed of processing are critical, first-class quality can hardly be expected when vegetables are purchased through normal retail channels for freezing at home. This does not apply to vegetables bought direct from a grower, transported coolly and quickly, and frozen as soon as home is reached.

CHOICE OF VEGETABLES

Nearly all vegetables freeze well, with the exception of salad vegetables which lose their crispness. Family preferences will therefore help the freezer owner to decide the quantity of each to freeze. It is not economical to use freezer space for vegetables with a long season, e.g. cabbage, or for vegetables that store well by other means as most root vegetables do. However, baby carrots and turnips freeze well and are useful for garnishes. Pieces of full grown marrow are hardly worth freezing, but baby marrows or courgettes are attractive. Onions develop off-flavours and their use is best restricted to made-up dishes where they should be used sparingly.

SOME RECOMMENDED CULTIVARS

The list below gives some cultivars recommended for home freezing by commercial seed houses and most generally available in the U.K. (There is no guarantee that the cultivars listed have been fully tested as to their suitability for home freezing.)

Beans, Broad	Aquadulce, Aquadulce Claudia, Masterpiece, Green Long Pod
Beans, Dwarf	Masterpiece, Processor, Tender Green, The Prince
Beans, Runner	Achievement, Crusader, Kelvedon Marvel, Scarlet Emperor, Streamline
Beetroot	Boltardy
Brussels Sprouts	Citadel, Peer Gynt

37

Carrots	Amsterdam Forcing, Chantenay Red Cored, St. Valery
Cauliflowers	All The Year Round, Barrier Reef, Canberra, Dominant, Snowball, South Pacific
Celeriac	Globus
Courgettes	Early Gem F1
Peas	Dark Skinned Perfection, Early Onward, Feltham First, Gradus, Hurst Green Shaft, Kelvedon Wonder, Onward, Pilot Improved
Spinach	New Zealand
Sprouting Broccoli	White Sprouting, Purple Sprouting
Sweet Corn	Early King, Kelvedon Glory
Tomatoes	Gardeners Delight

PREPARATION

The general procedure for washing and preparing vegetables for cooking is used for freezing. Special requirements are noted under individual vegetables. Clean vegetables do not require washing and prolonged soaking spoils their quality. To draw out grubs soak vegetables for a maximum of half-an-hour in water containing 1 level dessertspoonful of salt per quart. Grading to size gives an even result.

BLANCHING

Most foods are frozen without any special preliminary treatment, but for nearly all vegetables blanching or scalding is recommended. In this treatment, the vegetables are briefly heated to inactivate enzymes which, if unchecked, would gradually bring about quality and vitamin loss during frozen storage. Blanching is carried out by scalding the vegetables in boiling water.

The object is to heat the vegetable sufficiently to inactivate the enzymes and then at once to cool it rapidly to avoid softening. Only small quantities of the vegetable can be satisfactorily blanched at a time. A large pan containing 4 litres (about 7 pints) of boiling water is suitable for 250 g ($\frac{1}{2}$ lb) vegetables at a time. The vegetables are placed in a wire basket or a bag of muslin or nylon mesh which is plunged into the boiling water containing 1 level teaspoonful salt per quart of water. Alternatively, the vegetables can be placed directly in the boiling water and after blanching they are strained through a colander over a bowl. The water can be returned to the pan for further use. If the vegetables float, they must be pushed under the water. The vegetables inevitably cool the water to a certain extent and it is important that it should return to the boil within one minute. A lid on the saucepan will hasten re-boiling. If the heat is insufficient to allow this, a smaller quantity of vegetables must be used for subsequent batches. If a metal basket is used, it should be heated in the blanching water before putting in the vegetables. The time of blanching varies with the size and type of vegetable and should be exactly calculated from the re-boil. Where two blanching times are given in the Table, the shorter is for small young produce or small pieces, and this should be increased to the longer period for larger samples. As soon as the period is over, the vegetables should be cooled in really cold water. The cooling time should be approximately the same as the blanching time which is sufficient to cool the vegetable below cooking temperature without leaving it long enough to become soft.

Blanching water can be used up to 6 or 7 times for the same kind vegetable. There is no need to boil fresh water for each batch and, in fact, it is generally agreed that vitamin C retention is improved after the first one or two batches.

Fresh cooling water is needed for each batch. When cooling is completed, the vegetable is drained in a colander, not dried, and then packed.

BLANCHING TIMES

Vegetable	Preparation	Blanching time after water reboils (mins)	% waste
Artichokes (Globe) whole	Use when young and tender Discard outer leaves, cut off buds at top and trim base to a cone shape	8–10	
fonds (bases)	Remove all the leaves, keep under cold water. Add 2 teaspoonsful citric acid or 2 tablespoonsful lemon juice to 2·5 litres (4 pints) blanching water to prevent darkening	4–5	
Asparagus	Scrape off lower bracts, cut to suitable length for package. Grade stems according to size. A rigid pack protects heads	2–4	
Aubergine (Egg plant)	Cut in half lengthways or peel and cut into 10–25 mm ($\frac{1}{2}$ to 1″) slices or cubes. Acid may be added to blanching water as for Artichokes	5 3–4	
Beans Broad	Pod and grade to size. Discard starchy, over-mature beans	3	40–70
French	String if necessary and cut off ends. Best picked small and frozen whole, otherwise cut in chunks	2–3	5–12 stringless 18–35 others

Vegetable	Preparation	Blanching time after water reboils (mins)	% waste
Runner	String and cut off ends. Cut into chunks about 10 mm ($\frac{1}{2}''$) wide. If thin slices are preferred, flavour will be improved if these are cut after blanching	2–3	18–35
Beetroot	Choose beet up to 50 mm (2″) in diameter. Remove skins after blanching and cooling. Larger beetroot may be cooked, cooled, skinned and diced or sliced, but tend to be watery in texture when thawed	5–20	
Brussels Sprouts	Small compact sprouts must be chosen. A small cut made into the base of the stem in preparation will ensure even cooking	3	18–35
Cabbage	Worth freezing in areas where green vegetables are scarce for much of the year. Select fresh, well-hearted white or Savoy heads. Remove outer leaves and large stalks. Cut into 10 mm to 20 mm ($\frac{1}{2}$–$\frac{3}{4}''$) wide slices, wash quickly if necessary	1–2	
Carrots	Choose small, even, well-coloured carrots. Skin after blanching, pack whole. Larger carrots may be frozen sliced or diced. Fully mature carrots are not recommended	5	15–45
Cauliflower	Choose compact heads and break into florets about 50 mm (2″) across. Small whole heads, up to 150 mm (6″) across can be frozen. If discoloured by brown spots of iron compounds, this can be counteracted by dipping in a weak citric acid solution immediately before freezing (0·2 g citric acid (2 × 100 mg tablets) per litre (2pt) of water)	3	25–42
Celery	If required for subsequent cooking, crisp, tender stalks may be frozen. Clean carefully, pull off any strings and cut into 25–50 mm (1–2″) lengths	2	
Corn-on-the-Cob	Avoid starchy or undeveloped cobs. Remove husk and silk. Cobs wrapped individually in foil and frozen can be baked and served in it	4–6	35–50
Corn – whole grain	Scald the cobs and then cut off the grain with a sharp knife. The best parts of unevenly developed cobs can be used		65–80
Courgettes	Cut when 10–15 cm (4–6″) long. Do not peel. Freeze whole, halved or in thick slices	2–3 whole 1½ halved or sliced	
Mushrooms	Cultivated mushrooms are widely available throughout the year and therefore freezing is usually unnecessary. Fresh, young field mushrooms should be well cleaned, peeled and the stalks trimmed.	None	

Vegetable	Preparation	Blanching time after water reboils (mins)	% waste
	Mushrooms should *not* be blanched as this toughens them. Either rinse in clean water and freeze while still damp, or sauté in butter before freezing		
Peas Shelled	Young sweet peas are essential for a good product	1–2	50–70
Mange tout	Where the whole pod is eaten, it is particularly important to use young produce. Add mint when cooking, if liked	2	
Peppers	Use in firm, plump condition. For storage over 6 months, blanch. For shorter storage the colour will be brighter if unblanched	3	
Potatoes New	Raw blanched potatoes are not recommended. Choose small, even-sized potatoes. Scrape, slightly under-boil in salted water, drain, pack and freeze		
Chipped	Use a good chip cultivar (Majestic). Peel potatoes and cut into even chips. Allow to soak for $\frac{1}{2}$ to 1 hour in cold water, drain and dry. Fry in a basket in deep fat or oil until the chips become translucent, but not coloured. Spread out to cool and then freeze		
Crisps	Prepare as for chips but cut crisps very finely. A potato peeler may be useful for this. After frying the crisps until translucent, remove the frying basket, re-heat the fat and continue frying until the crisps are golden brown. Spread out to cool and then freeze		
Spinach	Wash very thoroughly. Pull out stem and also main vein. Scald in small quantities	2–3	5–35
Sprouting broccoli	Purple and white sprouting broccoli freeze well and green sprouting (Calabrese) is outstandingly good. Use only tender sprigs and cut them to suitable lengths for the package. As the heads are tender a rigid pack is advisable	3	
Tomatoes	Frozen tomatoes are too soft to be used in salads but firm-ripe small or medium tomatoes can be frozen whole or halved for use in cooked dishes. Tomato pulp from skinned, liquidized or cooked tomatoes freezes well and is usually preferred		

Vegetable	Preparation	Blanching time after water reboils (mins)	% waste
Mixed Packs			
Macedoine	Peas, carrot cubes, French beans and sweet corn. Prepare and blanch the vegetables separately and after cooling make up the assorted packs		
Root vegetables	A mixture of root vegetables is often required for soups or sauce. Prepare and slice or cube carrot, turnip, swede, celery, etc. to choice. The same blanching water can be used throughout, but each kind of root should be blanched on its own. Cool, mix and pack in suitable *small* quantities. The inclusion of onion is not recommended	3–4	
Herbs	Culinary herbs should be frozen when young. Gather early in the morning while they are dew fresh. There are three usual methods of preparation for freezing:-		
	1. Wash the sprigs, pack and freeze. This is a suitable method for parsley		
	2. Wash the sprigs, remove the leaves from the stalks. Chop the leaves finely and pack into small containers. Alternatively, blanch the leaves for $\frac{1}{2}$ minute before chopping. Blanching darkens the colour but it will not deteriorate on storage. Unblanched herbs tend to become brown after a few months' frozen storage		
	3. Prepare the herb as for 2. and add a little water. Turn into an ice cube tray and freeze. When frozen, the cubes of herbs are removed from the tray, wrapped and replaced in the freezer. For mint, vinegar can be substituted for water.		
	Methods 1. and 2. are suitable for use in stuffings and method 3. for use in sauces		

Although it is customary to pack, seal and label before freezing, some freezer owners prefer to have a free-flowing pack. For this the drained blanched vegetables are spread out on a clean metal tray such as a Swiss roll tin and placed in the freezer in contact with the evaporating coils. Peas will take about 4 to 6 hours to freeze, sprouts 6 to 8 hours. As soon as the vegetables are frozen, they must be transferred to a pack and sealed. Food left in the freezer unwrapped will desiccate so packing must not be delayed.

PACKING AND FREEZING

It is sometimes asked whether fully-cooked vegetables can be frozen to avoid blanching. This can be done, but the quality of the product falls far short of a similar product blanched before and cooked after freezing.

RECOMMENDED STORAGE PERIOD

Blanched vegetables keep their quality in a freezer at −18°C or below for 12 months. Most would be of high quality for a longer period, but there is no advantage in longer storage for a crop that can be replaced annually. The few vegetables recommended for freezing unblanched (mushrooms and peppers) will begin to show quality loss after about 6 months, although they will be acceptable to most palates for up to 1 year. Most other vegetables frozen unblanched show quality loss at about 4 months and it depends on the fineness of the consumer's palate how soon the developing off-flavour becomes unacceptable. For a comparison of storage life when blanched and unblanched, (See table on p. 45).

UTILIZATION

The majority of vegetables are cooked direct from the frozen state. For 500 g (1 lb) vegetables allow 300 ml (½ pint) water and 1 teaspoonful of salt. Bring the water to the boil in a small lidded saucepan, and add the vegetables. If they are frozen in a block, separate them as they begin to thaw. When the water re-boils, lower the heat to give a gentle boil and replace the lid on the saucepan. The cooking time will be about two-thirds the time taken by similar fresh vegetables. Drain, toss in butter, if liked, and serve in a warmed dish. Exceptions are:

Asparagus: As with fresh asparagus, it is desirable to support the heads out of water so that they can cook in the steam while the thicker stalks are in the boiling water.

Aubergines
Courgettes } When using a recipe for these vegetables stuffed and baked, they can be used from the frozen state
Peppers

Corn-on-the-Cob: This should be taken from the freezer and left in its wrapping until thawed or partially thawed before cooking. Thawing can take place overnight in a refrigerator, or at room temperature for 5–6 hours, or in a bowl of slightly warm water for an hour.

Peas: An alternative method is to put the peas in a saucepan with 25 g (1 oz) butter, 1–2 tablespoonsful of water and cover and cook gently until the water has evaporated. Add seasoning and serve. With either method a little sugar and a sprig of mint can be added during cooking.

Potatoes: New potatoes should be placed in a saucepan with a few table-spoonsful of water, 25 g (1 oz) butter and a sprig of mint, and gently heated. The water should evaporate during the heating, which will complete the cooking of the potatoes. Remove the mint, and add a small cube of frozen parsley or some fresh chopped parsley. Shake the pan gently to distribute butter and parsley evenly over the potatoes. If time permits, the appearance of new potatoes can be improved by thawing in the pack before heating.

Chipped potatoes should, if possible, be allowed to thaw in the pack for 2 hours at room temperature, or for $\frac{1}{4}$ hour in tepid water. If they must be cooked from frozen, a few at a time can be dropped into hot fat, but this is not recommended because of the excessive bubbling and steam. The chipped potatoes are ready when golden brown, and they should be drained on absorbent paper and seasoned with salt before serving.

Potato crisps are best spread out on a baking tray to thaw, and re-heated in a moderate oven. If thawed at room temperature they lack crispness, but they must be watched in the oven as they quickly darken.

Mushrooms: Plain unblanched mushrooms can be cooked from frozen with a little butter and seasoning in each cap under a moderate grill. Mushrooms sautéed before freezing, can be gently re-heated in a small lidded saucepan.

Spinach: Cook from the frozen state with one tablespoonful of water in the saucepan. Keep pan covered and use low heat until the block begins to thaw. Drain very thoroughly and add butter and seasoning before serving.

Herbs frozen in the sprig: If the pack is removed from the freezer and immediately rubbed between the hands, a quickly prepared 'chopped' herb is produced and the stalk can be taken out quite easily. Cold hands and quick action are essential for success.

TABLE 4

Approximate storage times of frozen vegetables at −18°C (0°F)

		Time of storage	
	Blanching time	Unblanched	Blanched
Beans			
Broad	3 min	3 weeks	12 months
Dwarf (French)	3 min	4 months	12 months
Runner	3 min	1 month	12 months
Brussels Sprouts	3 min	3 days	12 months
Carrots	5 min	12 months	12 months
Peas	2 min	6–9 months	12 months
Peppers	3 min	3 months	12 months
Spinach	3 min	12 months	12 months
Sweet Corn	5 min	1 month	12 months

CHAPTER 7

Fruit

COMPARATIVELY FEW fruits are frozen commercially for the domestic market. This scarcity gives added appreciation of the home frozen product. For a true fresh flavour out of season, no other method of preservation can surpass freezing. Good results depend on the fruit being picked in perfect dessert condition on a dry day, handled carefully, kept cool and frozen as quickly as can be. Shallow containers are essential for soft fruit to prevent crushing and over-heating. Temperatures are often high at picking time and fruit should be given every opportunity to cool. If fruit has to be left in a car, it should be parked so that the fruit is shaded from the sun's heat.

CHOICE OF FRUIT

Most fruits can be frozen with considerable success. Any loss of quality is usually in texture and this is particularly noticeable in strawberries and dessert pears. All light-coloured fruits darken through oxidation, and to overcome this special precautions are taken which in no way detract from the flavour. With stone fruit, it is best to remove the stones in fruit to be stored for over 6 months, because of the strong almond flavour that develops, though this is enjoyed by some.

SOME RECOMMENDED CULTIVARS

The list on p. 47 gives some cultivars that have scored well in palatability tests in the South of England, but this list is by no means exhaustive. Many seedsmen's catalogues give recommendations which can be of particular value for their own locality, wherever it may be in the United Kingdom.

PREPARATION

Leaves, twigs and unsound fruit should be discarded. Clean fruit should not be washed but where washing is necessary it should be quick. For soft fruit it is best to put a small quantity in a colander and gently pull the colander through clean cold water. With raspberries and other fruits likely to contain insects or maggots, spread the fruit on a large dish or sheet of clean greaseproof paper and leave for an hour, after which time most of the creatures will have crawled out and can be removed.

All fruits can darken during frozen storage because of oxidation and enzymic activity. This is less noticeable with dark fruit and presents little problem within twelve month's storage. Light fruit suffers a

Apples	Bramley's Seedling, Grenadier, Lane's Prince Albert
Apricots	Moorpark
Blackberries	Large ripe wild berries or Bedford Giant, Himalaya Giant
Blackcurrants	Baldwin, Boskoop Giant, Seabrook's Black, Wellington XXX, Westwick Choice
Blueberries	Jersey
Cherries	Any dark red, Governor Wood, Morello (acid)
Damsons	Merryweather, Shropshire Prune or most varieties
Gooseberries	Careless, Golden Drop (dessert), Leveller, Whinham's Industry (red)
Loganberries	Thornless (use fully ripe and dark red)
Mulberries	Use fully ripe. The core can be eliminated by pulping and sieving the fruit
Peaches	Hale's Early (freestone)
Pears	Not recommended for freezing as the fruit will lose its texture
Plums	Not particularly recommended whole, but can be halved in syrup or stewed. Remove stones. Belle de Louvain, Jefferson's Gage, Victoria
Quince	From common quince tree
Raspberries	Glen Clova, Lloyd George (dark), Malling Admiral, Malling Jewel, Malling Promise, Norfolk Giant, September
Rhubarb	Victoria
Strawberries	Cambridge Favourite, Cambridge Vigour, Redgauntlet, Cambridge Prizewinner, Royal Sovereign, Cambridge Rival (jam)

marked darkening, particularly in the less acid fruits. This could easily be arrested by blanching as for vegetables, but the fruit would lose its fresh appeal and other methods are adopted. Where fruit is acceptable in stewed form, the colour is retained by stewing, which destroys the enzymes and disperses the intercellular air, before freezing. If quickly stewed, the retention of ascorbic acid should be better than in fresh material where the enzyme that degrades ascorbic acid is unchecked and can therefore lower vitamin C content during frozen storage.

ANTIOXIDANT ADDITIVES FOR LIGHT-COLOURED FRUIT

In the past, lemon juice has been used to preserve colour but to be at effective strength its flavour was apt to mask the flavour of the fruit. Now ascorbic acid (vitamin C) is commonly used. It has the advantage of being more effective than lemon juice or citric acid and at the same time boosting the vitamin C content of the pack. Ascorbic acid can be bought in crystalline form or in tablets of various concentrations. For the housewife relying on domestic scales it would be impossible to weigh the minute quantity required in crystalline form. One level teaspoon holds about 3000 mg crystalline ascorbic acid which is sufficient for 2·75 kg (6 lb) fruit or for 1·5 litres (3 pt) of syrup. For smaller quantities of fruit, tablets are more suitable; 3 × 100 mg tablets of ascorbic acid with 200 ml water or syrup should cover 300 g fruit (or 6 fl. oz. syrup to 10 oz. fruit). The ascorbic acid should be added to the syrup just before use; it is easier to crush the tablets with a spoon and dissolve them in a little of the liquid before adding to the main bulk. For dry sugar packs, up to 500 mg ascorbic acid can be allowed for 500 g (1 lb) fruit. The tablets should be crushed and dissolved in 1 tablespoonful of water. This is used to sprinkle the fruit which is then rolled in caster sugar to give a fine coating before freezing.

Fruit can be frozen in various ways and the usual methods are given below.

PLAIN

The clean prepared fruit is packed in suitable quantities, sealed, labelled and frozen. A free-flowing pack can be produced by spreading the fruit in a single layer on a metal tray and freezing in the coldest part of the freezer. It is important to pack and seal the fruit as soon as it is frozen, to avoid desiccation (4–6 hours).

This quick method is suitable for dark fruits, whole marmalade oranges, and gooseberries for subsequent cooking. Enzyme activity is uncontrolled and the basic darkness of the fruit masks the discolouration that occurs slowly on storage. The acidity of gooseberries helps to retard darkening but as they will be cooked before eating they might with advantage have been stewed before freezing.

IN DRY SUGAR

For this the fruit should be coated with sugar which will form a protective glaze. Caster sugar is the usual choice and 60 g per 500 g fruit (2 oz per lb) is sufficient to coat the fruit, but more can be used according to family taste, or added on thawing. The fruit and sugar should be gently mixed and left in a covered bowl for up to 2 hours until the sugar has drawn sufficient moisture from the fruit to produce a coating of syrup. If the fruit has been washed, the moisture will help to speed up this process. Otherwise, a tablespoonful of cold water may be sprinkled on the fruit before adding the sugar. With this method it may occasionally be noticed that during frozen storage the fruit appears to be increasingly covered with a mould-like formation. This is due to a type of crystallization and generally disappears on thawing. This condition is mentioned here as it can alarm the unsuspecting housewife. It is entirely harmless and has no connection with mould.

This method is suitable for all fruits except apples, apricots, pears and peaches which would be liable to discolour. Enzymic activity is uncontrolled but the dry sugar coating protects the fruit from oxidation to some extent.

IN SUGAR SYRUP

Syrup forms a good barrier between fruit and air and therefore prevents oxidation and discolouration. The strength of the syrup can be adjusted to taste. The following table gives the proportions for various strengths of syrup:

TABLE 5

Strength of syrup		Sugar to add to water		Yield of syrup approx.		Sufficient for fruit (normal pack)	
		500 ml	1 pint				
	%	g	oz	ml	fl.oz	kg	lb
Weak	17	100	4	550	22	0·8	2¼
Medium	38	300	12	675	27	1·0	2¾
Heavy	45	400	16	750	30	1·1	3
Very Heavy	60	750	30	1 litre	40	2·5	4

A 'normal pack' of 500 g consists of 300 g fruit to 200 ml syrup. There is no need to follow these proportions strictly but they will be found to give a good balance. An excess of syrup spoils the fresh appearance of the fruit when served. The weaker strengths of syrup are used for fruit for subsequent cooking, the heavier strengths for dessert fruits. The correct method of preparing syrup is to bring the water to the boil in a clean lidded saucepan, add the sugar, stir to dissolve, return to the boil and boil for 2 minutes. Cool before use, or chill if possible. For light fruit, half fill the container with cold syrup and drop in the fruit as it is prepared. If so wished, unrefined sugar, honey or syrup can be used, but the true flavour of the fruit will be masked.

In Sweetened Fruit Juice

Where fruit is in plentiful supply, the juice can be extracted from over-ripe samples and water and sugar added to taste before using the liquid in place of sugar syrup for fruit freezing. Fruit of the same kind is used in most cases but there is scope for experiment, e.g., strawberries in red currant juice, pears in blackberry juice.

Pulp or Purée

Mis-shapen fruits can be pulped or puréed either raw or cooked, sweetened or unsweetened, for use after freezing in desserts, ice creams, etc.

Stewed

Fruit to be eaten stewed will take up less room in the freezer if cooked before freezing. It should be sweetened to taste preferably before freezing and should be slightly undercooked to allow for softening when thawing.

Jam-making

When soft fruit is being frozen for subsequent jam-making, etc., sugar up to 20% of the weight of the fruit may be added before freezing and a note of this must be made on the label. It is not advisable to add sugar to blackcurrants or plums because of its toughening effect on the skins.

Pie Filling

For plate (double crust) pies mix 1–2 teaspoonsful of cornflour or arrowroot depending on the juiciness of the fruit, with the sweetening for each 250 g ($\frac{1}{2}$ lb) fruit. This will prevent the fruit juice making the bottom crust soggy when the pie is made up and cooked.

Packaging

With tender fruits a rigid container is preferable and is essential for light coloured fruits that must be kept submerged in syrup with a wad of crinkled greaseproof paper. Firmer, dark coloured fruits, pulps and purées may be frozen in polyethylene bags. Remember to leave a headspace in syrup packs.

Preparing Fruit for Freezing

Fruit	Recommended method
Apples, sliced	Choose a good cooking variety. Peel, core, cut into even slices and blanch for 1½–3 minutes until pliable. Then cool quickly and pack

Fruit	Recommended method
	in a compact block of the required size. A little weak syrup can be added. It is advisable to take one or two slices at first to test the correct blanching time, as this varies with cultivar and state of ripeness.
Apples, pulp	Choose a good cooking variety. Peel, core, slice, and cook in minimum water until tender. To obtain a drier pulp, the slices may be blanched for up to 4 minutes, and beaten smooth. Add sugar if required. Cool before freezing.
Apples, purée	Either of the above pulp methods may be used for purée which must be passed through a sieve before freezing.
Apples, baked	Cook partially and cool before freezing; reheat to complete cooking.
Apricots	Fully ripe apricots should be wiped with a clean cloth and frozen either whole or preferably halved and stoned. They should be submerged in heavy syrup containing ascorbic acid for freezing. Alternatively, they can be pulped, sweetened, cooled and frozen. For jam-making, freeze fruits whole coated with sugar. The kernels will be easy to remove after freezing.
Blackberries	Really ripe wild fruit has the best flavour. Cultivated fruit tends to be acidic. Remove stems and leaves, rinse quickly in cold water and drain. Freeze in medium to heavy syrup or dry sugar using about 100g per 500g (4 oz. per lb) fruit.
Bilberries	See Blueberries.
Blackcurrants	Not used as dessert, but well worth freezing raw or cooked, or as purée. Pack plain or in dry sugar. For subsequent jam-making, a 1 minute blanch (see p. 45) has been found to give an improved jam. After blanching, pack fruit and cool package in icy water before freezing.
Blueberries	This cultivated fruit, or wild bilberries or wortleberries freeze well and keep their

Fruit	Recommended method
Blueberries *continued*	bloom. The cultivars Bluecrop and Jersey are recommended, the former having particularly good size berries. Rinse in clean water if necessary and freeze in medium to heavy syrup.
Cherries	White cherries are not recommended. Ripe red or black cherries should preferably be stoned and frozen in medium to heavy syrup. The juice which runs out when stoning should be allowed to drip into the syrup as this will conserve the flavour. Morello or other bitter sweet cherries freeze well for subsequent use in pies.
Damsons	Freeze whole plain or pulped, or make into pie fillings. The stoning of damsons is tedious, so they are usually frozen whole and used within six months.
Elderberries	Choose good sized berries and remove from the stalk. The berries are improved if given a $\frac{1}{2}$ minute blanch in boiling water and then cooled before freezing. This wild berry may not be everybody's choice and is best used from the freezer in conjunction with apple or blackberry.
Figs, green	Select fruit ripened on the tree, wash and cut off stems. The fruit can be peeled, frozen whole or sliced, submerged in medium to heavy syrup, preferably containing ascorbic acid.
Gooseberries	It is not advisable to freeze fully ripe dessert fruit. Full grown, firm berries can be topped and tailed and frozen plain, but as they are always cooked before eating it is better to stew or purée them before freezing to save valuable freezer space. If required for subsequent jelly-making there is no need to top and tail.
Grapefruit	These are worth freezing when there is a cheap supply of good juicy fruit. Peel carefully to remove all pith and cut into segments free from skin and pips, add sugar to taste and allow it to dissolve before freezing. Leave a small headspace in the container.

Fruit	Recommended method
Grapes	These tend to be very soft when thawed and are best used to give variety in a fruit salad. Freeze seedless grapes whole but seeded types should be cut in half to remove seeds.
Greengages	Can be treated as light plums, but for dessert use are better bottled.
Lemons	Whole fruit can be frozen.
Lemon rind	Wash ripe, blemish free lemons, dry and grate peel. Store in small containers. Rancidity may be detectable if stored in the freezer for more than six months.
Lemon juice	Squeeze out juice, strain and freeze in small containers. If a considerable quantity is available, the juice may be frozen in the ice cube tray and then wrapped in individual cubes.
Lemon slices	Separate by a double fold of polyethylene or greaseproof paper. These freeze well and are useful in drinks. Squeezed halves can be wrapped and frozen and grated from frozen when required.
Loganberries	This tart fruit can be frozen when fully ripe in dry sugar or syrup, but for dessert use bottling is recommended.
Melons	When good quality fruit is in plentiful supply these are worth freezing. Cut in half, remove seeds and peel. Shape flesh into balls or cubes and freeze in heavy syrup. These are best eaten before fully thawed and preferably mixed with other fruit.
Mulberries	This fruit must be fully ripe and very dark in colour. Choose succulent berries and freeze in heavy syrup. The core of this fruit is hard and can be sieved out if a purée is prepared.
Oranges	As for grapefruit or lemons.
Peaches	Select firm ripe peaches. To remove skins, dip the fruit in boiling water for $\frac{1}{2}$ to 1

Fruit	Recommended method

Peaches
continued

minute and then cool at once in cold water. Prepare the fruit quickly to prevent discolouration. Peel, cut in half and remove stone. Submerge fruit in heavy syrup containing ascorbic acid. If preferred fruit can be sliced. White or yellow fleshed peaches may be used and the fresh flavour is well preserved in the freezer.

Pears

The texture of pears tends to soften in the freezer, although the flavour is well retained. Ripe but not over-ripe pears should be used. Peel, halve and core the fruit and submerge at once in heavy syrup containing ascorbic acid. A 1 minute blanch in boiling syrup will help to maintain the whiteness of the fruit without impairing its texture if reasonably firm fruit is used. The fruit can be quartered or sliced if preferred. Cooking pears may be frozen, after cooking until nearly tender. Thawing will complete the softening. If cloves are added, they should be used sparingly as spice flavours tend to enlarge.

Pineapple

The fruit on sale in England at an economical price is rarely of good enough quality to produce first-class results. Prime ripe pineapple freezes well, but should be used within about three months as it develops an off-flavour.
Peel the fruit, remove the core and eyes. Cut into slices, cubes or wedges and freeze in heavy syrup. Retain any juice that escapes in preparation and add it to the syrup. Trimmings can be roughly chopped, sweetened and frozen.

Plums

Plums soften and discolour on thawing if not used immediately. This is particularly evident with light coloured varieties and least noticeable with black cultivars and with damsons. Fruit must be ripe but firm. Remove stalks and rinse fruit if necessary. If fruit is to be stored more than 4–6 months, the plums should be cut in half, the stones

Fruit	Recommended method

removed and the fruit submerged immediately in medium to heavy syrup. For dessert use, bottling is recommended. Plums can also be pulped for subsequent use in puddings or made into pie fillings.

Raspberries   Probably the most satisfactory of all frozen soft fruits. Choose fully ripe fruit and do not wash unless necessary. The berries can be frozen plain or with dry sugar or in syrup. When coating with dry sugar care must be taken not to crush the berries. For a plain pack spread out the fruit in a single layer on a metal tray and freeze. As soon as the fruit is firm put into bags, seal and replace in freezer. Raw sieved sweetened raspberry purée is an excellent method for using very ripe or badly shaped fruits.

Rhubarb   Choose young pink rhubarb, wipe and cut into 2·5–5 cm (1–2″) lengths. A 1-minute blanch is recommended to retain colour and flavour. After cooling, the rhubarb can be frozen plain, coated with sugar or in syrup. Blanching is not essential. If rhubarb is a popular choice, the main crop sticks can be cut up, the 'strings' removed and the fruit stewed with sugar and the minimum of water or made into pie filling. Unless rhubarb is a family favourite, freezer space could probably be better used for more exciting produce.

Strawberries   Whichever method is adopted for this popular fruit, it must be remembered that the berries will be very flabby if allowed to thaw thoroughly before eating. Choose small to medium size fruit, ripe and well coloured, but not too soft. Hull the berries and rinse in cold water if necessary. The fruit can be frozen plain, with dry sugar or in heavy syrup. Some advantage in quality has been obtained by soaking the fruit in syrup for up to 4 hours before freezing. In the U.S.A. it is a usual practice to slice large berries

Fruit	Recommended method
Strawberries *continued*	before freezing but there are few English dishes that utilise strawberries in this way. Raw sieved sweetened strawberry pulp, preferably with added ascorbic acid, is recommended for utilising large fruits.

RECOMMENDED STORAGE LIFE

Pineapple should be used within 4–6 months, but other fruits will retain good quality for 12 months or longer. The addition of sugar prolongs high quality life so plain packs should be eaten first. As with vegetables there is no point in keeping a stock of a frozen seasonal crop beyond its next harvest.

UTILIZATION

For dessert use, the fruit should still be chilled when eaten. The unopened pack can be placed overnight in a refrigerator. This slow thawing keeps the fruit in good condition for several hours. If less time is available, 4–6 hours at room temperature will be sufficient to thaw a 250 g ($\frac{1}{2}$ lb) pack of fruit in syrup or sugar. Dry packs take rather longer. For greater speed the package can be floated in tepid water, but if left too long the result will be mushy.

Dry packs and uncooked purées should be thawed rather quickly to prevent undue darkening of colour. In all cases packs should not be opened until ready to serve.

To cook, dry pack frozen fruit should be put into a saucepan over gentle heat until the juice begins to run. It is advisable to moisten the pan with one or two tablespoonsful of water as a frozen pack can burn on the bottom of the pan. Once the fruit begins to thaw the heat can be increased. Syrup packs, stewed fruit and fruit purées do not need the addition of water, but the heat must be gentle at first.

PIE FILLINGS

For plate (double crust) pies the filling should be thawed before putting in the pastry case. However, the high sugar content speeds up the thawing rate and if the frozen pack of filling is removed from the freezer and put in a bowl of tepid water it will be ready for use in about 15 minutes. For fruit tarts with no undercrust very little thawing is necessary.

Purées are usually required cold and, unless sweetened, will take rather longer to thaw than a similar sized pack of fruit. Overnight thawing in a refrigerator is therefore recommended. Thawing time will vary with the size and shape of the pack and the room temperature, but for surest results, when time permits, overnight in the refrigerator is best.

JAM

For jam-making the frozen fruit should be placed in the jam pan with water if necessary. Freezing and thawing tends to soften the fruit and the quantity of water to be added can consequently be somewhat reduced. If no added water is required it is advisable to moisten the pan to prevent burning until the juice begins to run. The fruit is softened and the quantity in the pan reduced by about one-third before adding the sugar. If a proportion of the sugar was frozen with the fruit a corresponding reduction in the quantity added must be made. After the sugar is dissolved, the jam is boiled rapidly until setting point is reached.

MARMALADE

The bitter oranges could be thawed overnight and then prepared with the other ingredients. For speed, the frozen fruit together with any unfrozen citrus fruit can be cooked whole either in a saucepan with a lid (2–3 hours) or in a pressure pan ('HIGH' or 15 lb. pressure for 20 min.) and then prepared after softening. In this case it is advisable to return the pips to the pan for a further 5 minutes boiling to extract the pectin. The quantity of water required for 1·5 kg fruit is 3–3·5 litres (3 lb. fruit to $4\frac{1}{2}$–$5\frac{1}{2}$ pts) in a covered saucepan and 1·8 litres (3 pints) in a pressure pan. The rest of the procedure is as for ordinary marmalade making.

CHAPTER 8

Meat

MEAT IS to be found in most freezers and is frequently the main food stored. This links with the high proportion of meat eaten in the national diet and has been accentuated by its rising price which may turn the freezer into a profitable storehouse for bulk purchases. Many freezers have been purchased solely with this benefit in mind.

SELECTION AND HANDLING

Few people start with the live animal but the importance of high quality can scarcely be overstressed. In addition the treatment of the animal pre-slaughter, together with skilled handling, speed, and correct temperature through slaughter, evisceration and cooling are factors that play an important part in the maintenance of quality. Offal is removed and trimmed during evisceration and this should be frozen as soon as it is thoroughly cooled. Cooling is undertaken at a temperature between 0° and 2°C (32° and 36°F) and then the cooled carcase should be allowed to mature by hanging in a temperature of 1°–4°C (34°–39°F) with a humidity of 85–90%. After hanging for some days meat is cut into joints as required. This is the stage at which many customers see the meat for the first time.

Butchery is a skilled trade and meat an expensive food, so the would-be bulk purchaser should seek advice from a reliable source. The family butcher is in many cases the best person to consult, as he knows the family pattern of eating, is anxious to satisfy a regular customer and can offer price cuts comparable with other sources. Other good suppliers are well-known in their own areas and the more experienced freezer owner may purchase direct from the abattoir. Extreme care should be exercised before making an apparently very favourable purchase from a previously unknown source. With the high price of meat experience can be dearly bought.

There are two main ways of buying meat in bulk. First, a whole carcase or a side of pork or lamb or a quarter of beef may be offered cut into joints. By this method, joints of different quality will be obtained, some suitable for grilling or roasting and some for casseroles or for stewing. The second way is to select the required number of cuts of a required quality. This enables the customer to buy, for example, fillet steaks or breasts of lamb according to taste and purse. On the whole, the purchase of a whole side or quarter forces the housewife to be adaptable and enterprising, but it is as well to find out in advance from the butcher or from a recipe book, the cooking quality of the cuts. The price per pound quoted for sides and quarters will indicate to the discerning customer the proportion of first quality meat likely to be included, and a decision must be reached about the acceptability of the cheaper cuts. A hindquarter of beef will yield about 20% grilling meat, 45% roasting meat and 35% meat suitable for stewing or mincing. A forequarter, on the other hand, will give only a small quantity of good grilling meat, 20% of roasting meat of high quality, 50% slow or pot roasting meat and 30% stewing or mincing meat. Attractive and appetising dishes can be made from cheaper cuts, but they may need more lengthy treatment than some busy housewives are prepared to give.

Where high grade cuts are bought in bulk, it is necessary to be strong-minded to save money. Better eating without increasing cost is usually the standard attained.

CUTTING

Some freezer owners are keen to undertake the cutting up but this is better and more economically performed by a butcher. Naturally there is a charge for this time-consuming service but it is usually money well spent. For the enthusiast, lamb and pig carcases can be tackled at home if a large strong table, good knives and sharp saws are available in a cool room. This is still the practice in some rural areas where, by long tradition, the home pig has been dealt with on the premises. It is hardly worthwhile to face the necessary outlay on special implements where these are not already to hand. Beef is a much more difficult proposition and should be left to a butcher to cut. When dealing with local suppliers, cutting can be adjusted to meet home requirements, a facility not necessarily available from wholesale suppliers. Space is saved in the freezer if the meat is boned, but this does away with the traditional appearance of some joints and care is needed in labelling so that confusion does not arise. Boned joints look very similar to the untrained eye.

PREPARATION

Raw meat should be kept cool, clean and covered from the time it leaves the supplier until it is put in the freezer, and this period should be as short as possible. Meat should not require any further trimming, but any excess fat may be trimmed if necessary.

PACKAGING

Where there is too much meat to put into the freezer at one time, the joints to be held over to the next day should be bagged, but not sealed, and put into the refrigerator. If they have to be kept in a cool pantry, the opening of the bag should be put under the joint to prevent access by flies. In either case, the air is expressed and the bag sealed immediately before putting into the freezer the following day.

Where wrapped frozen meat is bought, it should be taken home in an insulated container and placed in the freezer at once. It is as well to inspect wraps so that any that are torn can be quickly overwrapped with a polyethylene bag and sealed. Packaging is particularly important as 'freezer burn' will develop on meat in a punctured pack. Butchers' wraps may be of a self-sealing material which looks rather fragile, but is, in fact, usually quite adequate for the treatment the meat should receive.

JOINTS

The irregular shape and presence of bone in some cuts makes the packaging a little difficult, but most joints can be put in a gussetted polyethylene bag or given a butcher's wrap (p. 34) of sheet polyethylene or other freezer wrapping paper. It is important to press out as much air as possible before completing the seal. Where there are projecting bone ends, these should be sawn off if possible, otherwise they must be covered with foil or layers of greaseproof paper before wrapping. With a very uneven joint it is advisable to overwrap the package with stockinet (mutton cloth) or clean paper. This protective layer prevents fracture of the wrap and consequent dehydration.

SMALL CUTS

Individual chops, steaks, sausages, slices of liver, kidneys, must be separated by a double strip of greaseproof paper or polyethylene before wrapping. If this is not done, the pieces of meat will freeze together into a block and, unless thawed, it will not be possible to separate the quantity required. Several small packs of the same kind can be put in a 'sausage' of stockinet or polyethylene tubing and tied between each portion. This keeps packs, say, of liver together.

KINDS OF MEAT

BEEF, PORK AND LAMB FREEZE WELL

Large quantities of frozen lamb are imported and there are many queries about its suitability for home freezing. Frozen carcases can be cut up into small joints with an electric saw, wrapped and placed, still frozen, in the home freezer without quality loss. If the meat is allowed to thaw and then re-frozen, the quality will be less succulent, although the safety should not be at risk if cut as soon as thawed and then re-frozen. A reputable salesman of meat for home freezing would not sell *thawed* frozen meat for this purpose.

OFFAL

These perishable products should ideally be frozen as soon as chilled after slaughter and are therefore better purchased already frozen.

TRIPE

Prepared tripe freezes well.

MINCED MEAT AND STEWING MEAT

These are more quickly ready for use if minced or cut up before freezing, but seasoning should not be added before freezing, as salt accelerates the development of rancidity. Care must be taken in packing to express as much air as possible.

CURED MEAT

As salt accelerates rancidity, cured meats have a much shorter recommended freezer storage period than the same meats unsalted.

For salt pork, a mild cure can be obtained by freezing the meat fresh. One week before it is required, it should be thawed and placed in a pickling brine for 3–5 days, depending on its thickness. It is then held in a refrigerator for a day or two before cooking. The first cooking water should be drained off as soon as it boils and replaced with fresh water. Cooking time is 20–25 mins. per 500 g (1 lb).

BRAWN

This can be frozen but the jelly may weaken somewhat on thawing. As this is a highly perishable food, it should be frozen in suitable quantities to be consumed at a sitting. Bones can be frozen but it is better to make a concentrated stock with them and freeze it. The ice cube tray makes a convenient container and the stock cubes produced can be individually wrapped for use as required.

FREEZING

If the supplier offers an appropriate freezing service, this is to be recommended, as all the prepared, wrapped cuts can be frozen without delay. Wrapped unfrozen meat will not benefit from a journey home, particularly in warm weather, whereas similar joints frozen to −20°C (−4°F) or below by the supplier, tightly stacked and wrapped in newspaper will be less affected by the journey to the home freezer. Some suppliers provide refrigerated transport home for frozen meat. Commercial freezing equipment will deal with the whole order at one time whereas the home freezer has only a limited freezing capacity (see p. 22, Ch. 4). This can be stated broadly as 1 to 1·5 kg food per 30 litres (2 to 3 lb per cu. ft.) of total freezer capacity. From this it will be realized that a 560 litre (20 cu. ft.) freezer may not be able to freeze more than 20 kg (45 lb) food in 24 hours. A bulk purchase of meat for a home freezer of this size might well be 60 kg which is 3 full freezing loads. The home freezing options in this situation are either to freeze on three consecutive days 20 kg at a time or to put all the meat in at once. The first option is to be preferred, provided that storage at around 4°C (40°F) is available for the meat held over. Domestic refrigerator cabinet temperature will be satisfactory for this period, but few refrigerators have sufficient capacity to deal with these quantities. It is important on a three-day rota to freeze offal and small cuts on the first day and follow on with large cuts and joints. The meat should be wrapped but not sealed during the holding period and it must be remembered to complete the seal before freezing as meat dehydrates very quickly if exposed to air at freezer temperature. This holding period should not be regarded as an extension of the maturing period as it does not improve quality.

If the other option is chosen and the three-day freezing load is put in all at one time, the freezing rate will be much reduced with the possibility of excessive drip on thawing. The choice of options may be difficult but this loss of quality is preferable to possible spoilage or safety risks in holding meat for three days at 15°C (60°F) or more if no cool storage is available.

In exceptional cases, there may be a need to freeze large quantities of meat, even up to the full freezer capacity. This cannot be undertaken in a single load as the inevitably slow rate of cooling could allow time for spoilage. A third of total capacity should not be exceeded and two, preferably three days should elapse before introducing another load. With large quantities, the extra cost of commercial freezing is compensated by the assurance of safety and quality.

TABLE 6

Recommended maximum storage period for fresh meat held at −18°C (0°F) or below

	months
Beef Lamb }	12
Pork Veal }	9
Stewing meat, cut up	6
Whole mild cured ham Brawn }	3
Vacuum packed rashers or other bacon joints	$2\frac{1}{2}$
Minced meat Offal and tripe Smoked bacon }	2
Sausages Unsmoked bacon }	$1\frac{1}{2}$
Home-wrapped rashers	2–4 weeks

It will be realized that a freezer can be completely loaded with *already frozen* food as the refrigeration required to keep frozen food at −18°C (0°F) is about one-eighth of that required to freeze it.

All home freezers should reach the level of freezing performance outlined in this chapter. Some may be rather better as, for example, fan-assisted types, but the overall variation between models is small compared with the rapid freezing performance of commercial methods. This is not to denigrate the home freezer which produces highly acceptable meat and meat products and on this alone earns a place in many households without consideration of other foods.

UTILIZATION

JOINTS

Where time allows joints should be thawed slowly without removing the wrap. In a domestic refrigerator, a 1–1·5 kg (2–3 lb) joint will take up to 24 hours to thaw. The more solid the joint, the longer the time required to thaw and it is wise to allow 16–20 hours per kg (8–10 hrs per lb). The slow rate of thawing of joints or any 'solid' frozen packs is due to the immense amount of 'cold' they bring into a small refrigerator which is constructed to cool food not to warm it up. Therefore thawing time is more realistic if the meat is left at cool room temperature 10°C (50°F) for 6–8 hours per kg. A current of air speeds thawing and the *cold* air from a fan can be directed onto a wrapped joint. Meat which is thawed slowly will keep its condition if it is not used as soon as thawed whereas meat at room temperature should be moved into a refrigerator as soon as it is thawed both for quality and safety. In either case cooking should not be unduly delayed. Thawed meat can be cooked by any appropriate recipe for the type of joint or cut. Any drip in the wrap should be included in the cooking process. It can be poured over meat to be roasted or grilled, or added to stews or casseroles. With good meat and good method drip should be small in quantity but it is worth utilizing because of its content of water soluble vitamins of the B group and minerals.

COOKING MEAT FROM FROZEN

ROASTING

This is an asset where thawing has been overlooked.

If cooked directly from the frozen state, the colour will be paler and the texture will be tougher than for meat thawed before cooking. There will be no significant difference in juiciness, whether or not it is thawed before cooking, unless it is cooked in a roasting bag, in which case the meat not cooked in a bag will be juicier. No sealing crust forms on meat cooked in roasting bags, and this leads to a continuous loss of moisture and a dryness in the meat. There is no significant difference in overall acceptability between meat cooked directly from the frozen state or thawed first. The important factor is to get sufficient heat for safety throughout the joint. With fresh meat, time scales have been developed to achieve this according to weight, but with frozen joints the depth and balance of lean, fat and bone, play their part. For safety, an accurate meat thermometer should be used and placed in the thawed joint so that it records the temperature in the centre of the thickest part. Such thermometers cost about £1·50 and are available from many kitchen shops and chains of frozen food suppliers. A little practice is required to find the right position for the thermometer in the joint so that it is registering correctly and can be read easily.

Recommended temperatures at the centre of the joint are:

	°C	°F
Beef	74	165
Lamb } Pork }	85	185
Veal } Ham }	77	170

When cooking meat from frozen, a little water should be put in the roasting tin. Cooking times at 190°C (375°F) Gas Mark 5 will be about double the time for similar fresh joints. Rare cooking is not recommended and the thermometer readings above give medium, not overcooked, results.

AUTO-COOKING

A joint fresh from the freezer can be unwrapped, placed in a roasting tin, with 10 mm ($\frac{1}{2}$ in.) water, and put in the cold electric oven to auto-cook later in the day. An electric oven would not be a good place to leave thawed or fresh meat for several hours, but the thawing joint will be safe because of its low temperature. The degree of thaw will depend on the size of the joint and the temperature in the kitchen but the reduction in the final cooking time will be up to 15 mins. per kg (2 lb) for a small joint and less for a larger one.

With gas, the heat from the pilot light makes it inadvisable to leave joints in the oven for a lengthy period before cooking.

GRILLING

Chops and steak, etc. can be prepared from frozen, although thawing takes only 2–3 hours at kitchen temperature.

To grill 10 mm ($\frac{1}{2}$ in.) thick steaks from frozen, give full heat on each side for 3 minutes and than a further 2–6 mins. each side, according to the degree of 'doneness' required. There is no need to fear the initial effect of high heat on frozen meat as the ice reduces its burning powers, but as thawing proceeds lower heat should be used.

SAUSAGES burst if cooked from frozen.

STEWING MEAT AND MINCE can be cooked gently from frozen if time does not allow for thawing.

RE-FREEZING

The freezing, thawing and re-freezing of uncooked meat (or any other food except ice cream) can be done in an emergency but is bound to have some adverse effect on the food quality and nutritional value as extra 'drip' is inevitable. The chief hazard is to the safety of the food and this risk can be minimized if the food is (1) thawed in a refrigerator with a maximum temperature of 5°C (41°F), (2) the necessary adjustment to the food (probably cutting into joints) is made as soon as it is thawed, and (3) it is re-wrapped and returned to the freezing compartment in the freezer at once. Thus no opportunity is given for spoilage micro-organisms to multiply. Unfortunately in a situation where there could be risk, the need for attention to temperature and timing is sometimes overlooked and therefore for safety's sake the process is not advocated. The position is different where foods are thawed, cooked in some form and then re-frozen, as any increase in spoilage micro-organisms (due to delay or too much warmth) should be destroyed by the cooking.

DOG AND CAT FOOD

Any animal meat unfit for human consumption must not be prepared with family utensils, and must not be kept in the freezer. This cannot be overstressed in the interests of health and hygiene.

Other animal meat, preferably cooked, should be wrapped and sealed in day-size portions and stored in the freezer in a separate basket or bag. It must be fully thawed before feeding and if this has been overlooked the bag can be put into hot water to hasten thawing—at the expense of quality, which will not be noticed by a hungry animal. Any drip in the bag should be included in the feed.

CHAPTER 9

Poultry

BULK SUPPLIES of frozen chicken are always available, either whole or jointed, and can be transferred easily from shop to home freezer with minimum trouble and expenditure. Frozen turkeys and ducklings are now available all the year round, with guinea fowl also on offer in many areas. All of these may be regarded as useful freezer fillers, particularly to the town dweller. Provided the original birds were of good quality and the transfer from shop to home freezer was rapid, the final product will be very palatable.

Many country dwellers wish to freeze their own poultry. Birds will be reared for table, or more probably for egg production. In either case, the birds will reach a stage when they are ready for killing, and the freezer will enable the glut to be utilized over a period.

POULTRY

The birds available are likely to be surplus young cockerels, or hens of $1\frac{1}{2}$ or more years. Cockerels can be killed at 'broiler' weight, but with hens the preference is for a bird of about 2 kg (4–5 lb live weight).

Two-year-old cull hens may be fat and older birds can be very fat indeed. The keeping quality in the freezer will diminish as the fatness increases.

With young birds discolouration in the bones can be unattractive. This is due to the haemoglobin in the bone marrow which develops a dark colour on thawing. It is in no way harmful and cannot be prevented entirely.

DUCKS AND GEESE

The type and amount of fat in these birds reduces their high quality storage life. A Michaelmas goose is less fat than one killed later. For present day tastes such a bird prepared and frozen in September may be preferred at Christmas to one left to fatten for 2–3 extra months and then eaten fresh.

It is advisable to kill waterfowl when they are free from pin feathers. The removal of these increases plucking time immensely and they spoil the down which is a valuable commodity. Given cool conditions a goose will be improved by hanging for up to a week before evisceration, depending on its size, but 1–2 days is sufficient for ducks. During this period the internal temperature should be below 4°C (40°F).

TURKEYS

The unexpected gift of a large turkey can be an embarrassment to a small family. If tradition can be overridden, the carcase may be cut in half, one half roasted fresh and the other half frozen for use later. Even more radical treatment is to remove the legs and freeze them for later casseroles. The whole bird can be cooked and half or parts frozen, but meat cooked from the freezer is usually preferred to large portions cooked before freezing. Turkeys improve by hanging at 4°C (40°F) for up to a week between killing and use or freezing.

PIGEONS

It is usual to hang wild pigeons for 2–3 days in a cool place but tame pigeons do not benefit from hanging longer than overnight.

KILLING AND PLUCKING

Birds should be prepared in the usual way. An overnight fast with a plentiful supply of water should precede killing. Dislocation of the neck is the usual home method of killing poultry, but whether the neck is dislocated or the bird is stuck after stunning it is essential to drain the blood by holding the bird in an inverted position—legs up, head down—during plucking. The sooner the bird is plucked after killing the easier it will be to remove the feathers. When the bird has cooled before plucking it is sometimes recommended to dip it into hot water to loosen the feathers, but this cannot be advocated for birds to be stored.

Birds should be clean plucked, except for geese and ducks where the feathers need not be removed from the last joint of the wing, as these are cut off.

After plucking the birds can be shaped, but it is more usual to fold the wings behind the body and hang the bird by the legs. Given cool, pest-free storage, carcases are improved by hanging one to two days for 1·5–2 kg (3–4 lb) chicken and duckling, five days for large hens and cockerels and a week for turkeys and geese. Greening round the vent will occur in birds not starved before killing, or during mild and humid weather. Only careful preparation and refrigeration will ensure a high quality carcase. Hanging must always be carried out before dressing. Drawn birds should be wrapped and frozen without delay.

DRESSING AND PACKING

Birds are drawn in the usual way, care being taken to keep the flesh clear of intestinal contamination. The internal cavity should be inspected, especially when eviscerating hens, to ensure cleanliness. If a bird has been well drawn there should be no need to pass a cloth or run tap water through the cavity. Neither of these procedures does anything to enhance the quality. However, if there is extraneous matter in or on the carcase it must be removed by washing carefully.

Giblets should never be packed inside the bird unless wrapped. Where poultry is likely to be stored for more than three months, it is better to store giblets separately or to cook them and freeze the resultant stock. Onion and seasonings should be used sparingly. They can be added when re-heating to make gravy.

The carcase should be tied compactly, and any bone ends protected with foil or greaseproof paper before packing. A polyethylene bag makes a good wrap, as it is easy by an upward movement of the hands to press out the air. There is an infinite variety of sizes of polyethylene bags. Although it is economical to buy the one or two sizes most commonly used, a small supply of large bags is useful for turkeys, geese and large fowls.

Chicken livers are a delicacy and can well be frozen separately or made into a pâté and frozen. It is much better to freeze the livers and make the pâté as required. The high fat content of pâté reduces the length of its acceptable life in the freezer and the texture is less smooth after thawing. These are minor points however, and it is in many cases more useful to have the finished pâté in the freezer. It should be packed in quantities likely to be consumed at a meal.

Duckling, geese and turkeys are usually frozen whole, but chicken can be cut into joints, depending on requirements. Small birds can be cut into two halves and very small ones can be spatchcocked; this is done by cutting out the backbone and the wishbone. A press of the hand will flatten the carcase and in this form the bird can be grilled or fried after thawing. This treatment gives a very flat space-saving pack.

STUFFING

Stuffing birds before freezing is not recommended and there are two good reasons for this. In the first place, the herbs and seasoning used

TABLE 7

Maximum storage period at −18°C (o°F) or below in good polyethylene packaging

Chicken	1 year	
Hens	9 months	
Turkey		
Ducks		Heavy gauge
Geese	6 months	polyethylene
Pigeons		required
Giblets	3 months	

develop off-flavours in about three months, and the storage time of the bird is thereby curtailed. Second, and more important, is the safety factor—an unusual hazard with correctly handled frozen foods. Stuffing, by its make-up and handling, is a product likely to contain a high number of micro-organisms, and it is possible that in the final cooking the heat would not penetrate sufficiently to destroy these.

UTILIZATION

Slow thawing of the unopened pack in a refrigerator is recommended, allowing 10–12 hours per kg (5–6 hours per lb). Less time in proportion will be required for large birds, but a 7 kg (15 lb) turkey will take a full three days to thaw. Suitable thawing instructions should be found on the pack of bought frozen poultry. Thawing at room temperature requires 4–6 hours per kg (2–3 hours per lb) but this can be speeded up by placing the package in a draught which will reduce the time to about 1½ hours per kg (45 mins per lb).

GAME AND RABBIT

The usefulness of a freezer is fully realised in a sportsman's house. Game makes an occasion, but it can become unrewarding if eaten daily to clear a good bag. Hence the appreciation of the freezer to spread the pleasure over a period of time.

The eating quality of game depends on its age, the skill of the shot and on correct hanging. The entrails of deer, hare and rabbit should be removed as soon as possible after killing and the deer's head should be removed. All game should be transported in cool conditions and then hung to mature. This process is important as it gives time for the meat to become tender. Tenderising is linked with decomposition and it is largely a matter of personal taste to decide when there is the right balance between tenderness and flavour. The following table will indicate the period to be allowed:

TABLE 8

	For immediate use (days)	For freezing (days)
Wild duck and rabbit	1–2	1
Pheasant, grouse, partridge	6–7	5–6
Hare	7–9	5–7
Venison	10–12	8–10

A rule of thumb test for birds is to pluck a few feathers from above the tail. If these come away easily the bird is ready for eating. For freezing slight resistance should be felt.

Where much game is handled, provision will usually have been made for hanging. The temperature should be about 4–7°C (39–45°F) and any rise above this will reduce the period. There should be no strong air currents as these will dry the carcases. Flies and pests must be excluded. For those with no facilities, it is advisable to seek the co-operation of a butcher with good cold rooms, otherwise poor conditions may ruin the food. Game birds are hung by the neck, and deer, hare and rabbit by the back feet. A stick across the deer's belly will enable air to reach the inside of the carcase.

At the end of the hanging period, the carcase is prepared by plucking, or skinning, evisceration and dressing as required. The carcase or joints are then wrapped as for meat or poultry and frozen. It is advisable to state the intended use of the bird on the label, as this will prevent joints of casserole quality from being roasted.

If the blood from the hare has been retained, it should be frozen as soon as possible, or the hare can be jugged before freezing. With a small family this is the recommended procedure as the completed recipe can be divided into three or four portions, each sufficient for one family meal, one to be eaten right away and the others frozen. Forcemeat balls should not be included, but added before serving.

TABLE 9

Recommended maximum storage period at −18°C (0°F) or below

As the meat has fully matured before freezing, enzymic activity tends to be more rapid than with other meats	
'Fat' types (water birds)	6 months
Lean types	9 months

UTILIZATION

Thawing should be in the unopened pack as for poultry or meat, in a refrigerator allowing 10–12 hours per kg (5–6 hrs. per lb). When thawed, the required recipe can be followed as usual.

CHAPTER 10

Fish

FRESHNESS OF food for freezing is nowhere more important than for fish. Although commercially frozen fish can be quickly transferred to the home freezer without loss of quality, it cannot be recommended to buy fresh fish from a shop for home freezing. The length of time from catching to freezing must be as short as possible. For fillets the whole fish should pass through rigor before they are cut. The skeleton holds whole fish in shape during rigor but fillets shrink badly if cut pre-rigor.

WHITE FISH. These freeze well.

OILY FISH freeze well but have a shorter high-quality storage life in the freezer than white fish because the higher fat content can give rancidity.

TROUT. Sometimes frozen whole ungutted, but it is preferable to remove the gut. As it is usual in many recipes to present the trout whole, the intestines can be drawn out at a gill rather than by cutting into the flesh.

SHELL FISH; OYSTERS; SCALLOPS. Keep cool after removal from beds or the sea. Prepare and freeze as soon as possible. Clean the shells by washing. Open and remove the whole 'body'. Discard the inedible parts but take care to retain the liquor. Wash the meats in salted water (2 dessertspoons to the quart) but do not leave them soaking for longer than 3–4 minutes. Pack in 1-meal portions in a rigid container, cover with the natural liquor and keep submerged with crumpled greaseproof paper under the lid.

CRABS; LOBSTERS. Use without delay from the live state. Cook before freezing for 20–30 minutes, according to size. Lobsters should be plunged into boiling water alive but crabs must be inactivated before cooking to avoid the shedding of limbs. This is best done by placing in fresh water at a temperature of about 30°C (86°F) for about 2 hours before cooking.

SHRIMPS; PRAWNS. Cook for 2–6 minutes, according to size, in boiling salted water. Shell and remove the veins before freezing it for use within about 8 weeks. For longer storage or for larger species such as scampi, it is recommended that only the tail containing the meat, and the large claws if any, should be retained. Wash in lightly salted water and freeze in small rigid packs. They can then be cooked and shelled after removal from the freezer.

PREPARATION

Fish should be prepared as required for use. The scales should be scraped off, the intestines removed and the fins trimmed. The cavity should be washed out with clean water.

For whole fish, of single portion size or larger, each one should be packed to exclude air in polyethylene, sheet foil or other freezer wrapping material. Polyethylene tubing is particularly useful as it can be purchased in various diameters, and lengths can be cut as required. The fish is placed in the tubing which is sealed off at either end.

A traditional method of wrapping whole fish is to coat it in ice. To achieve this, the fish is placed in the coldest part of the freezer until it is frozen. It is then quickly dipped in a pan of nearly freezing water and returned to the freezer. The dipping is repeated once or twice until a continuous coating of ice covers the fish. This ice wrap adheres closely to the skin and protects the fish from quality loss by oxidation. As the ice is likely to chip, an overwrap is recommended and this must be put on quickly so that the ice coating has no chance to thaw.

For fillets or steaks, it is important to place a double fold of greaseproof paper or polyethylene strip alternately with the fish so that the required number of pieces can be removed. Fillets of white fish can with advantage by placed for up to half a minute in salted water (1 tablespoonful of salt per pint) before wrapping. This has been found to improve the texture.

The preparation of shell fish is dealt with above, according to kind. In all cases there must be a good seal to the pack to prevent desiccation.

TABLE 10

Recommended maximum storage period at −18°C (0°F) or below

White fish	4 months
Oily fish Salmon, Trout Oysters, Scallops }	3 months
Crab and Lobster (cooked)	2 months
Shrimps (cooked)	2 months

UTILIZATION

Whole fish should preferably be thawed before cooking but single portion sizes can be cooked gently from frozen.

It is normally quite satisfactory to leave a large fish in a *cool* kitchen to thaw overnight. It should then be placed in a refrigerator after thawing if it is necessary to keep the fish for a few hours before cooking.

Fillets can be cooked from frozen as they are very thin, but it is advisable to cook them gently at first. The thickness of steaks varies and it is best to thaw thicker ones in their wraps at room temperature for half an hour.

Scallops can be cooked gently from frozen, as can oysters if they are wanted cooked. If oysters are to be consumed raw, they should be eaten as soon as thawed and any left over should not be kept in their raw state.

Fish is a highly perishable food and particular care should be taken over its use, whether fresh or frozen.

CHAPTER 11

Dairy Produce and Fats

MILK

THE EASY availability and bulky nature of milk makes it an uneconomical choice for home freezing. In an emergency, dried or U.H.T. (Long Life) milk is more useful, although homogenized milk gives a very even result after freezing.

CREAM

Excellent results can be obtained with frozen cream, provided that the right procedure is followed. The milk fat content should not be below 40%. The statutory minimum milk fat content of grades of cream on sale are:

Double cream	48%
*Whipping	35%
Single	18%

*Whipping cream sold in this country may contain 38–42% fat.
Double cream and some whipping creams, therefore, are suitable for freezing but single cream would separate and is not recommended. A good result can be obtained by mixing two parts of double with one part of single cream and this is more economical than using all double cream. Alternatively, a little milk can be used to dilute double cream; rather less than one-quarter the volume of the cream will give a suitable blend.

When cream is bought from a shop or roundsman it will most probably have been pasteurized. This makes for safety and also for better texture. Home-produced cream can be pasteurized by standing the vessel of cream in a pan of boiling water. The cream is gently stirred until it reaches 70°C (160°F) and is then removed from the heat and cooled. Such fresh cream should be left covered to mature at 5°C (40°F) for 1 to 2 days before freezing. The main cabinet of a refrigerator is the right temperature for this.

To give a good final texture cream should be *slightly* whipped before freezing and, if acceptable, the addition of a little sugar (1–2 teaspoonful per 250 ml (½ pint) before whipping will add final smoothness. Cream can conveniently be frozen in cream cartons. Only a small headspace is required but the lid should be secure, otherwise overwrapping with a polyethylene bag is recommended.

It is useful to have cream rosettes ready for use in the freezer. To prepare these, sweeten and fully whip double cream (48% fat), which may be diluted but not below 40% fat. (This is thicker than some creams sold as 'whipping cream', which may be only 35% fat). Pipe rows of

74

rosettes of various sizes on the *inside* of the lid of a shallow tin, or preferably a plastic box. Keeping the lid inverted, place the box in position and freeze. If no suitable box is available, a clean baking tray can be used; the rosettes are frozen uncovered and transferred to a container when firm. This transfer must be quick, to ensure that the slight thawing does not spoil the outline of the rosettes. Clotted cream loses its characteristic texture if frozen and, similarly, very thick double cream becomes somewhat 'tacky'.

TABLE 11

Maximum recommended storage time at −18°C (0°F) or below

Double cream Whipping cream }	6 months
Clotted cream	6 months but texture spoilt
Cream rosettes	3 months

UTILIZATION

Frozen cream is best thawed in the refrigerator and is improved by whipping before serving. For piping, it should be treated as fresh cream. Frozen cream rosettes should be lifted on a knife and placed as required while still firmly frozen. They will have thawed sufficiently in $\frac{1}{2}$ to 1 hour, depending on kitchen temperature.

YOGURT

As this is widely available and can be stored for several days in the domestic refrigerator, there is usually no reason to freeze it. Flavoured yogurt containing fruit and sugar freezes satisfactorily but natural yogurt is not recommended for freezing, as it has a lower total solids content and thus it becomes 'grainy' on thawing. Three months frozen storage should not be exceeded.

BUTTER, LARD AND MARGARINE

In some areas home-made butter and home-rendered lard are still produced. For most people there would be no point in freezing fats bought over the counter or from supermarket shelves. However, an occasional offer at reduced price may make a bulk purchase worthwhile. Fats freeze well, provided that they are well made, not stale when frozen, and not too salt. The best wrap is the one used by the manufacturer. If this is torn, it is advisable to overwrap closely with polyethylene. For home-made butter greaseproof closely overwrapped with polyethylene or polyethylene alone is recommended. Lard can be treated the same way, although it is often better to pour it into basins and cover them closely. Basins are wasteful of freezer space. It should, moreover, be remembered that hot lard will melt a plastic container.

TABLE 12

Maximum recommended storage period at −18°C (0°F) or below

Salted butter	3 months
Home-made butter	3–6 months
Unsalted butter ⎫ Lard ⎭	6 months
Margarine	12 months

UTILIZATION

The fat should preferably be thawed slowly at room temperature and can then be used as required. The texture may be considered somewhat granular.

CHEESE

The home freezer is extremely useful in prolonging the season for cheeses that have an annual peak period for quality and availability. There is little point in freezing hard cheeses that are always available. Soft cheeses must be in perfect condition before freezing. No further maturation takes place during or after freezing. Cottage cheese freezes particularly well.

Cheese dips freeze well and can be a great boon to the hurried cook. Cheese should be closely wrapped. Heavy duty foil is recommended as it can be pressed to adhere to the surface of the cheese and thus exclude air. A polyethylene bag is best for grated cheese.

TABLE 13

Maximum recommended storage period at −18°C (0°F) or below

Hard cheese ⎫ Cheese dips ⎭	3–4 months
Grated cheese	4 months
Soft cheese ⎫ Cottage cheese ⎭	6 months

UTILIZATION

Much of the criticism of the texture of frozen cheese can be countered by very thorough thawing. There is a tendency for hard cheese to become crumbly and for cream cheeses to be mealy or 'pebbly'. If cheese is held at cool room temperature for one to two days before eating, this effect will be minimised and full flavour will have returned.

Grated cheese from good dry cheese can be shaken from the bag as required without waiting for it to thaw. However, grated moist cheese will cling together and freeze in a piece. This makes it less instantly available and its moistness makes it less suitable in many recipes.

CHAPTER 12

Eggs

EGGS CANNOT be frozen satisfactorily without some previous treatment. There are many baked products which incorporate eggs and these freeze well. If therefore there is only a small surplus of eggs it may be easier to use them up in, for example, cakes which can then be frozen for later use. Another suggestion is to use them in lemon curd, as this will keep (without freezing) for up to six months providing a reliable recipe is used.

However, where there is a considerable surplus, they may be worth freezing. They must preferably be frozen not more than three days after laying. They cannot be frozen in shell.

Egg whites and whole beaten egg freeze very well indeed and require no special preparation, but yolks become gummy unless salt or sugar is added. It is necessary to have in mind the purpose for which these eggs will be used and to put down the packs in the right quantity for use. Some examples are:

2 whole beaten eggs with 2 teaspoonsful of sugar for cakes e.g. Victoria sandwich.

2 whole beaten eggs with 1 teaspoonful of salt for omelette or scrambling.

2 yolks beaten with 1 tablespoonful of sugar for biscuit making.

2 yolks beaten with 1 teaspoonful of salt for mayonnaise.

These quantities can be packed into small cream cartons and sealed, or the mixture can be frozen in an ice cube tray to provide the egg in convenient portions. In large scale work, large packs can be used but whatever size is used it should be right for a specific purpose. Thawed frozen egg should not be left around any more than fresh beaten eggs, and after thawing unused egg must be discarded, not re-frozen.

UTILIZATION

Eggs should be allowed to thaw before use. Eggs frozen with sugar thaw in $\frac{1}{2}$–1 hour at room temperature. Once the whole egg or yolk is

TABLE 14

Maximum recommended storage period at $-18°C$ ($0°F$) or below

Yolks beaten with salt or sugar	6–8 months*
Whites and whole beaten egg	1 year

*The shorter storage period is recommended where salt is used

thawed, it should be stirred well before combining with other ingredients. Whites thaw more slowly and can be used as required as soon as they reach room temperature.

CHAPTER 13

Ice Cream and Other Ices

THE POPULARITY of commercial ice cream with its wide distribution and everyday use, is to some extent due to the immense amount of care that is involved in its production. Apart from the method of making, temperature is critical both for quality and safety. The home freezer running at −18°C (0°F) or below keeps ice cream in good condition for up to three months, whereas in the frozen food compartment of a 3-star refrigerator one month is the recommended maximum, decreasing to a few days in a one-star refrigerator. The home freezer owner can purchase ice cream in bulk and thus make a considerable saving.

The commercial product has been mentioned first because of its high quality. Delicious ice cream can be made at home and frozen in the freezer, but texture may present difficulties due to the formation of ice crystals. A smooth creamy result is partly due to beating the mixture during freezing, and where this is omitted a fairly high proportion of whisked egg white will often be used in the recipe. With some recipes, the half frozen mixture is removed from the freezer and well beaten before final freezing occurs.

If much ice cream is made at home, the purchase of an electric ice cream machine should be considered. These machines hold about ½ to 1 litre (1–1¾ pints) of ice cream and maintain a steady beating during freezing. They are placed within the freezer and take the hard work out of producing ices of cream or sorbet type.

Most ice cream recipes that have been found satisfactory when frozen in the frozen food compartment of the refrigerator will give as good and probably better results when made in the freezer. Difficulty may be experienced with excessive ice crystals when very economical recipes or mixes are used.

Lollies can be prepared in lolly moulds or, at a pinch, in the ice cube tray. Sticks should be put in position before freezing and this needs rather careful contriving in an ice cube tray. Children can make a quick mixture with equal parts of fruit syrup (e.g. Ribena) or milk shake flavouring and water. This may separate a little in freezing but the flavour becomes more concentrated towards the centre which attracts

TABLE 15

Maximum recommended storage period at −18°C (0°F) or below

Ice cream Lollies, etc.	3 months

80

juvenile palates. Neat or diluted fruit juice can be used, but this entails the addition of sugar. For ice cream or any food to be served very cold, flavouring, sweetening or seasoning must be more definite than for food to be eaten warmer.

UTILIZATION

Portions of ice cream taken direct from the freezer should be allowed to stand at room temperature for 5 minutes before serving. This short period will improve palatability. Small children should not have ice direct from the home freezer as it could 'burn' the tender skin of the mouth.

ICE CREAM SHOULD NOT BE RE-FROZEN

Ice cream has a delicate structure. If its temperature is raised by over-loading the freezer with fresh foods or breakdown it will lose its characteristic structure and not regain it. It should in these circum-stances be discarded.

CHAPTER 14

Baked and Prepared Foods

ONE OF the great advantages of the freezer is its ability to preserve in good condition many made-up foods unsuitable for other methods of preservation. Before the introduction of home food freezers, most prepared foods had to be made shortly before consumption. Now, many meals, cakes, pastries, breads, etc. can be made when time permits and stored in the freezer for later use.

There are many books giving specific recipes for freezing. It is hoped in this publication to indicate how housewives can adapt their own recipes so that long-established 'family favourites' can find their place in the freezer. With the enormous range and variety of recipes, it is inevitable that some will escape mention and it is, therefore, worth repeating that no wholesome food will become dangerous as a result of freezing. Deterioration in quality (texture, colour, odour or flavour) may occur but there is no risk to safety if correct freezing procedures are followed.

FREEZING QUALITY

To ascertain the freezing qualities of food, a very simple test can be carried out, as follows: take 3 individual portions or slices of the ready-to-serve food, wrap each piece individually, seal and freeze them. After one month, thaw one sample and taste it, and deal similarly with the other two samples at two and three months. From this simple test it is easy to decide whether the food freezes well and whether quality deterioration can be detected as the period of storage increases. Very few foods will be wholly unacceptable and the degree of acceptability is a personal or family decision. Over-long frozen storage may give uncharacteristic colour and flavour changes but textural changes are largely due to the initial freezing process especially if this is slow. This textural breakdown can be seen in frozen baked egg custard.

BAKED PRODUCTS

BATCH BAKING OR 'DOUBLING UP'

Much has been written about setting a day aside for baking large batches of food for the freezer. Some households may be well equipped for this but for others lack of baking tins and limited oven capacity causes difficulty. The modern fan-assisted ovens make it possible to bake several trays of food at the same time but until these are in more common use, it is suggested that 'doubling up' or occasionally trebling recipes required for the day's menus will slowly but steadily build up freezer stock without undue extra time or effort. When the food is prepared, one portion is cooled for freezing while the other portion is eaten fresh. This fits in with the normal cooking routine and takes little extra time.

PACKAGING

As for all freezing, the wrap must be airtight. For tender baked products a protective box is necessary to prevent damage by other packs in the freezer. Lidded plastic or foil boxes of suitable dimensions are available but a baker's cake box will often serve the purpose at little or no cost. However, bakers' boxes are not airtight and either the baked goods or the box itself must be wrapped and sealed. With soft-surface cakes, the whole box should be wrapped to avoid smudging the surface of the cake.

FREEZING METHODS

Most baked foods, especially light cakes, stale rapidly at room temperature. It is therefore recommended that they should be frozen as soon as they have cooled sufficiently to feel *warm*, not hot, to the hand. They can be frozen unwrapped on a cake cooling tray. If the tray has long legs, it should be used upside down as the aim is just to break direct contact between the food and the freezing surface; a large air space would retard freezing. There are reservations about this method as it is not suitable unless there is a special freezing compartment which ensures that other frozen food will not be warmed up. It is not suitable for large loads because it would cause a rise in freezer temperature and excessive frost formation. It is essential to wrap and seal the food as soon as it is frozen, otherwise it will dehydrate. This method of freezing is particularly suitable for soft iced cakes.

Alternatively, baked products can be wrapped and sealed when hand warm and then frozen or, if preferred, put in the refrigerator for half an hour before freezing. Unwrapped cakes should not be cooled in the refrigerator as the drying effect would be as great as if they were left in the kitchen. Baked foods can be completely cooled before freezing without undue loss of quality but delay at this stage will give a dry product.

STORAGE PERIOD

Many baked products will keep their quality for long periods, but three months' storage should be ample for most requirements. These foods are bulky and make extravagant use of freezer space. They are not usually linked with seasonal produce so they do not need to be stocked up from harvest to harvest. A more profitable use of the freezer can be achieved if the stock of baked foods is rotated quarterly.

Most uncooked foods can be baked from frozen, although for dense packs pre-thawing is recommended to ensure ample heat penetration to cook to the centre without overcooking the surface. Ready-to-eat baked food can be thawed in the kitchen in two to eight hours, depending on the temperature of the kitchen and the size of the product. It can be thawed wrapped or unwrapped. In the latter case considerable condensation will be noticeable on the surface of the food but this will dry out as thawing proceeds. It is more hygienic to leave the food in its wrapper during thawing. Clinging wraps must be removed from soft-surface food while it is still frozen firm. Overnight thawing in a refrigerator is satisfactory. Bread and similar products can be thawed in the oven and served warm but subsequent staling will be very rapid. Pre-cooked pastry dishes are improved by 'refreshing' for a few minutes at 180°C (355°F) after they have thawed. Many cream cakes can be sliced more satisfactorily before thawing is complete.

FREEZING THE MAIN TYPES OF BAKED PRODUCTS

YEAST DOUGHS

FROZEN UNCOOKED: The living yeast cells on which this type of dough depends are adversely affected by freezing. If there is a special reason for freezing uncooked yeast mixtures, the ingredients should be mixed with minimum kneading and the dough then wrapped and frozen without allowing time for any rising. Some *small* rising may occur in the freezer before the dough freezes so a little space should be allowed when wrapping. Storage time should be as short as possible with a maximum of four weeks. Plenty of time must be allowed for the thawed dough to regenerate, as a large proportion of the yeast cells originally present will have been killed. The presence of many dead cells together with the necessarily protracted recovery time gives opportunity for the development of off-flavours and poor quality. These disadvantages can be overstated but it is generally accepted that yeast products cooked before freezing are more acceptable.

COOKED BEFORE FREEZING: This is the recommended method. The freshly baked products should be cooled, wrapped and frozen without delay.

Bread: Loaves can be frozen wrapped or unwrapped but it is essential to freeze them when freshly baked. The waxed paper covering on most bakers' bread is ample protection for up to two weeks but an airtight overwrap is required for longer storage. Short storage of home baked bread or a couple of loaves for an emergency is the usual family requirement. Long storage (over 3 months) is not recommended as the crumb shrinks away from the crust which becomes flaky so that slicing is impossible. Thawing of bread can be effected quickly in an oven at 180°C (355°F) for $\frac{1}{2}$ to $\frac{3}{4}$ hour. This gives a delicious freshly-baked result but any bread not eaten at once will stale very quickly. Slow thawing, either overnight in a refrigerator or for 4 to 6 hours in the kitchen, will produce a 'day old' result but will not stale any faster than fresh bread.

Sliced loaf: This is the most 'instant' frozen bread as individual slices can be toasted or fried direct from the freezer.

Rolls: For hot breakfast rolls, these can be deliberately under-cooked by 3 to 4 minutes before freezing so that the final 10 minutes at 180°C (355°F) direct from the freezer does not dry them too much.

Other yeast mixtures: Cook fully before freezing. They can be thawed in the oven if they are to be eaten hot.

PASTRY

Short, flaky, puff, flan: These all freeze well, especially when frozen before cooking. The amount of salt should be reduced. Three or four times the quantity normally required can conveniently be made but it should be wrapped and frozen in the required family size portions. Large blocks have to be partially thawed to cut off the required amount. This is time-wasting and it does not improve the quality of the portion that is returned to the freezer. If liked, the dish can be fully prepared before freezing, e.g., sausage rolls, or the pastry shaped for flan or vol-au-vent cases. Flan cases can be shaped in foil cases or in metal flan rings which can be removed once the pastry is frozen. Shaped pastry, such as flans, must be replaced in the mould before thawing. Glaze, if required, should be put on before cooking. Pastry can be cooked direct from frozen but if the filling requires considerable cooking, it is advisable to thaw first. It is not always advisable to thaw pre-baked pastry dishes in the oven as the pastry can become dry and chippy. However, pastry dishes cooked before freezing will be refreshed if they are warmed in the oven after thawing, otherwise the pastry may seem to lack freshness.

Choux: Shape and bake before freezing.

Hot-water crust: Shape, make up and bake before freezing. This pastry tends to be rather dull after freezing and it is recommended to rub a little margarine into the flour (25 g to 200 g flour or 1 oz. to 8 oz.) before mixing as usual with hot water and melted lard. Hot-water crust is used almost exclusively for meat and game pies. It is better to add the jelly stock as soon as the pie has thawed as the jelly liquefies if frozen and spoils the traditional appearance.

CHEESE STRAWS: Cook before freezing.

SCONES

As the dry rubbed-in mixture stores well in a covered jar in the refrigerator, it is of marginal value to freeze these. If shaped and frozen raw and subsequently baked from frozen, the scones will become rounded on top, so it is advisable slightly to under-bake them before freezing and to thaw them in the oven for about 15 minutes at 150°C (300°F). They are less attractive than freshly made ones but acceptable while warm.

CAKES

Although some cakes could be cooked satisfactorily from frozen, the general rule is to cook first, and to freeze as soon as hand warm (see p. 83).

RUBBED-IN MIXTURES: Plain foods lose some quality when frozen and this type of mixture scarcely merits freezer space. Large rubbed-in cakes with a good proportion of dried fruit are quite acceptable from the freezer.

CREAMED MIXTURES: Victoria sandwiches and similar mixtures freeze extremely well. As they should be frozen as soon after cooking as possible, it is advisable to add the jam filling just before serving. The two halves can be prevented from freezing together by a double fold of greaseproof or waxed paper or polyethylene.

Fruit cakes are very satisfactory but a reasonably rich fruit cake will keep in a tin for several months, a really rich cake for up to a year. However, if there are difficulties about this kind of storage, freezing will be an excellent substitute. Thawed fruit cakes tend to have a damp texture appreciated by most people.

Madeira or caraway cakes may have a slightly over-moist texture after freezing. Caraway may develop an off-flavour if stored more than three months.

SPONGES: It has been said that a fatless sponge is the one food than can increase in volume and quality due to freezing. This type of cake gives an excellent result.

GENOESE SPONGE: This mixture, a sponge enriched with melted butter, freezes perfectly and has the added advantage of being suitable for many uses. The mix can be flavoured and baked in various shapes to be used for iced fancies, Swiss roll, Russian cake, etc.

SWISS ROLL: This can be frozen complete but a more satisfactory result is obtained if it is rolled up on paper for freezing and the jam added after thawing. A butter cream filling can be added before freezing as this does not soak in like jam.

RUSSIAN CAKE: The cake can be prepared before freezing, with the alternate pink and white squares lightly put together with sieved jam and then the almond paste covering secured by a light coating of jam. This cake should be eaten within about two months as the cake contracts if stored much longer.

GINGERBREAD: This cake freezes well but the flavour of the ginger undergoes a slow change, which is scarcely discernible for two to three months but after that there will be an increasing pepperiness which is uncharacteristic but not usually commented upon unfavourably. A similar and perhaps less pleasant change can be found with cake containing cinnamon.

SHORTBREAD: If cooked before freezing the texture may be rather dry. A more buttery result is obtained if cooked from frozen but care is needed to ensure even baking.

BISCUITS: Can be satisfactorily cooked before or after freezing.

MACAROONS: The pleasantly tacky texture of these is somewhat enhanced by freezing.

MERINGUES: The extremely high sugar content of these confections enables them to freeze and thaw rapidly and without detectable change. They are ideally suited to freezing and can be eaten within a few minutes of removal from the freezer. Small button meringues make an 'instant' decoration for desserts. Large ones should be filled with cream after freezing.

ICINGS: Butter icing freezes well and can be put in or on a cake before freezing without risk providing the wrap is sufficiently firm to prevent damage. Glacé or water icing freezes satisfactorily but used on the surface of a cake it is inclined to crack when thawed.

Chocolate icing prepared with purpose made slab chocolate gives a good result although sometimes it is a little too firm.

Royal icing must be very carefully wrapped to protect it and to exclude moisture. Given these conditions it freezes well but it is usually adequate to keep it in a tin.

Almond paste or marzipan has a high fat content. It freezes well but storage should be limited to three months as bitterness may be detectable later.

CHAPTER 15

Prepared Meals

APART FROM the convenience of advance preparation of food for specific occasions, the freezer owner will be able to take advantage of current cut price offers and glut supplies for use later. Popular family recipes that are shelved because they require small quantities of many ingredients or depend on some rare commodity can be prepared in quantity when supplies are ample. Part can be eaten right away, the remainder packed in portions and frozen for later enjoyment.

PACKAGING

Where a frozen prepared food requires heating in a saucepan before service, a 'boil-in-the-bag' wrap can be recommended. Many of these are suitable for freezing and their use minimises washing up. They are usually one portion size which for family use can be expensive but have the advantage of heating quickly so that quality is retained. Where polyethylene bags are used, the frozen food must be removed before heating. Cold water run over the outside of the bag will loosen the contents.

Foods to be served cold or heated in the oven can be conveniently packed in foil dishes and over-wrapped if there is no adequate lid for the dish. Where it is wished to serve a prepared recipe in a particular serving dish, the food should be frozen in it and removed when firm so that it can, when required, be fitted back into the dish for final heating up. Care is needed as few types of serving dishes will stand sudden changes of temperature. A foil lining in the serving dish will enable the food to be removed easily when frozen and the foil can be taken off before returning the food for re-heating. Foil dishes for use with fruit should be protected by a lacquer coating, otherwise the fruit acid can cause pin holes. Manufacturers usually state if dishes are lacquered, so if they do not, it is safer to assume they have not been lacquered.

Although square-based rigid containers are more economical of freezer space than round ones, it may be convenient to use yogurt or cream cartons for freezing small quantities of sauce or garnish to accompany a prepared dish. A plastic container which has previously contained food can be washed and used in the freezer.

FREEZING METHOD

Most prepared foods will be hot and they must be quickly cooled before freezing. It is sometimes easier to portion them at once and then to cool before sealing. Special care should be taken to ensure cleanliness and quick cooling. The final cooling can be achieved by placing the food in the refrigerator for $\frac{1}{2}$ to 1 hour before freezing.

STORAGE PERIOD

Savoury prepared dishes usually contain salt and perhaps onions and spices, all of which reduce the retention of high quality in the frozen food. A maximum of three months' storage is recommended after which the food will become slowly less attractive although in no way dangerous. The discernment of the individual palate is the criterion.

Sweet or dessert dishes are usually less subject to the development of 'off flavours' but very light, whipped recipes tend to consolidate so that a 2 to 3 months maximum storage is recommended for them.

THAWING

Where the food is to be served hot, it can with advantage be gently heated from frozen, either in the oven or in a saucepan, depending on its type. 'Boil-in-the-bags' are placed direct in boiling water which should be ample to cover the food in the bag. It is easier to keep the lid off the saucepan during reheating, which is timed from when the water re-boils. For individual portions this is usually 15 minutes for fairly fluid ingredients, up to 20–25 minutes for a thick portion of meat. Where the frozen block of food is tipped direct into a saucepan it is advisable to have in the pan one or two tablespoonsful of stock, milk or melted fat as appropriate for the recipe to prevent burning. Gentle heat is essential until thawing is obvious. For heating in the oven, it is sometimes advisable to keep the dish covered but this depends on the nature of the recipe. Unless the dish is thermal shock-proof the food should be left in it to thaw before reheating. The shock of the frozen food will not crack the dish unless it is heated before the contents are thawed.

Prepared dishes to be eaten cold are conveniently and safely thawed overnight in a refrigerator.

FREEZING THE MAIN GROUPS OF PREPARED FOODS

The general rules in preparing made-up dishes for freezing are:
1. Avoid excess fat as this slowly develops a rancid flavour.
2. Use a minimum amount of salt as it accelerates the development of rancidity.
3. Omit or reduce onions as their flavour changes.
4. Be sparing with spices.

'STARTERS': Those suitable for freezing are usually uncooked natural foods which are best taken from the freezer and assembled with the addition of fresh garnish, if required. Aspic is best applied after thawing, as a suitable aspic for freezing has yet to be formulated.

Soup: Home-made cereal-thickened soups consolidate a little during freezing. This can be overcome by reducing the flour, etc. by one quarter, or more simply, by adding stock or milk to correct the consistency when reheating. Cream and wine are best added on reheating. Clear soups freeze satisfactorily. Finely cut vegetables in consommé must not be damaged during reheating. Egg liaison should be made on reheating as separation may occur if it is frozen.

Sauces, Roux Based: These sauces tend to thicken during freezing so it is advisable to reduce the amount of flour by 25 to 30% in both pouring and coating sauces. To reduce the risk of sauce 'cracking' on thawing, cornflour can be used to replace flour. Frozen sauces should be briskly stirred when reheated to restore their smooth texture. Flavoured sauces, such as béchamel, can conveniently be made in quantity and frozen in small units for use as required. Sauces with egg thickening break down when frozen and are not recommended.

Fish Dishes: Fish is quickly cooked and it is not improved by reheating. Made-up cooked dishes are therefore unusual. Kedgeree freezes very well and should be reheated under a foil cover in the oven. Unbaked Russian fish pie is satisfactory but must be thawed or practically thawed before baking. The surest method of thawing is to place the frozen pie in the refrigerator overnight. The pie can be baked before freezing but it is advisable to refresh the pastry by heating it in the oven after thawing. Fish cakes can be fried direct from the freezer but cause rather dangerous spitting of the hot fat, so care is necessary. They should not exceed 2–3 cm ($\frac{3}{4}''$–1$''$) in thickness so that they heat through in 10 minutes. If preferred, they can be grilled, in which case a small knob of butter or margarine on each will prevent drying out. Whether fried or grilled, the fish cakes should be turned over halfway through cooking.

Meat, Poultry, etc.: Whole cooked joints or birds are not improved by freezing. Slices of meat or poultry covered in well-flavoured gravy or sauce freeze satisfactorily for 1 to 2 months. Made-up dishes, casseroles, fricassées, etc. are well worth freezing. The visual effect is often more attractive if part of the recipe is prepared separately to enliven the homogeneous appearance of the rest. Without a little care in distinctive presentation the uniformity in appearance can detract from the excellence of the flavour of these dishes. With curry, the rice can be slightly undercooked, drained and frozen or freshly cooked while the frozen curry is being reheated. Frozen rice can be reheated in a covered dish in the oven or in a steamer. Beef steak and kidney pies and puddings are preferred cooked after freezing. Excess moisture in the filling should be avoided as this can spoil the undercrust. More gravy can be added before serving.

Desserts: 'Desserts from the freezer' conjures up a mental picture of exotic dishes, but most humble puddings freeze well, too. Milk puddings should be made with a sparing measure of cereal and they then give a good result. Where they are in regular demand for one member of the household, it is an economy in oven use to make several at a time. Cooked steamed puddings, either creamed mixtures or suet crust reheat well. The appropriate accompanying sauce can be frozen in a separate container.

Cold soufflés and home-made mousses freeze very well for up to a month but separate if stored much longer. If they are well protected, they can be fully decorated before freezing. They should be allowed to thaw in their wrap overnight or all day in a refrigerator as they lack flavour if served too cold. Hot steamed soufflés are not recommended for freezing either raw or cooked.

Pancakes freeze well and keep moist if one tablespoonful of oil is added per 100 g (4 oz.) flour. They can be frozen filled, but usually they are frozen flat with a fold of foil between each pair to prevent sticking together. To thaw and heat place the foil wrapped pancakes in a moderate oven.

Index

Other bulletins currently available

Copies of these Bulletins may be obtained from any of the Government Bookshops listed on the reverse of the title page (London mail to PO Box 569, London, SE1 9NH) or through our agents or booksellers—see Yellow Pages.

Prices are correct at the time of going to press; those in brackets include inland postage. All titles offered subject to availability of stock.

4	Bush Fruits, 1st edition, 1977	0 11 240527 4	£3·00	(£3·18½)
5	Fruit spraying machines, 6th edition, 1967	So 24–201–5–67	30p	(42p)
9	Beekeeping, 11th edition, 1973 (Reprinted 1976)	0 11 241209 2	75p	(84½p)
21	Home Preservation of Fruit and Vegetables, 13th edition, 1972 (Reprinted 1976)	0 11 241321 8	£1·00	(£1·22)
35	Lime and Liming, 7th edition, 1973 (Reprinted 1977)	0 11 241335 8	90p	(£1·02)
37	Silage, 10th edition, 1977	0 11 241337 4	£1·75	(£1·90)
38	Sex-Linkage in Poultry Breeding, 6th edition, 1966	SO 24–201–38–66	42½p	(57½p)
50	Commercial Rabbit Production, 9th edition, 1973 (Reprinted 1975)	0 11 241350 1	£1·50	(£1·62)
51	Narcissus Pests, 6th edition, 1970	0 11 240351 4	65p	(80p)
70	Ducks and Geese, 5th edition, 1973 (Reprinted 1977)	0 11 240370 0	£2·00	(£2·15)
97	Pests of Ornamental Plants, 3rd edition, 1974	0 11 240397 2	£3·65	(£3·94)
100	Diseases of Bees, 4th edition, 1969 (Reprinted 1976)	0 11 240400 6	£1·00	(£1·12)
107	Soils and Manures for Fruit, 4th edition, 1975	0 11 241407 9	£1·89	(£2·04)
136	Watercress Growing, 3rd edition, 1967 (Reprinted with minor corrections, 1968)	0 11 240436 7	27½p	(39½p)
138	Irrigation, 4th edition, 1974	0 11 241438 9	£2·75	(£2·97)
147	Electric Fencing, 5th edition, 1976	0 11 240656 4	80p	(89½p)
148	Incubation and Hatchery Practice, 6th edition, 1977	0 11 241448 0	£1·75	(£1·90)
152	Intensive Poultry Management for Egg Production, 5th edition, 1976	0 11 241115 0	£1·75	(£1·90)
156	Cane Fruits, 5th edition, 1975	0 11 241807 4	70p	(79½p)
160	Housing the Pig, 3rd edition, 1971	0 11 240460 X	£1·55	(£1·73½)
161	British Poisonous Plants, 2nd edition, 1968 (Reprinted 1976)	0 11 240461 0	£1·75	(£1·93½)
162	Sugar Beet Pests, 3rd edition, 1972	0 11 241462 1	£1·35	(£1·53½)
165	The Farmer's Weather, 2nd edition, 1964 (Reprinted with minor corrections, 1966)	SO 24–204–65–66	27½p	(42½p)
174	Poultry Nutrition, 4th edition, 1974 (Reprinted with minor amendments, 1977)	0 11 240474 X	£2·25	(£2·43½)
181	Control of Rats and Mice, 2nd edition, 1970 (Reprinted 1977)	0 11 240481 2	£1·50	(£1·62)
184	Squirrels, 1st edition, 1962 (Reprinted with minor amendments, 1975)	0 11 240484 7	£1·10	(£1·22)
193	Pig Husbandry and Management, 3rd edition, 1977	0 11 241118 5	£2·00	(£2·18½)
194	Control of Aquatic Weeds, 2nd edition, 1973	0 11 240494 4	£1·00	(£1·12)
198	Small Commercial Poultry Flock, 2nd edition, 1973 (Reprinted 1975)	0 11 241498 2	70p	(79½p)

199	Low Cost Dairying, 1970	0 11 240499 5	30p	(45p)
201	Hot Water Treatment of Plant Material, 2nd edition, 1972	0 11 240501 0	42p	(54p)
202	Water for Irrigation. Supply and Storage, 2nd edition, 1977	0 11 241519 9	£2·25	(£2·40)
204	Grass and Clover Crops for Seed, 1st edition, 1968	SO 24–207–4	39p	(54p)
206	Swarming of Bees, 2nd edition, 1973 (Reprinted 1975)	0 11 240506 1	70p	(82p)
207	Apples, 1st edition, 1972 (Reprinted 1977)	0 11 240597 X	£3·25	(£3·54)
208	Pears, 1st edition, 1973	0 11 240508 8	68p	(86½p)
210	Organic Manures, 1st edition, 1976	0 11 240510 X	£1·10	(£1·22)
212	Climatic Environment of Poultry Houses, 1st edition, 1976	0 11 240748 X	£1·10	(£1·22)

Standing Orders

Did you know that HMSO Books on various subjects can be supplied on Standing Order? If you have an account with us, we can send them to you as they are published. There are over 3,500 series and subject classifications to choose from such as all publications on

Beekeeping (X01.05.00)

Control of Weeds (X01.06.12)

Farm Produce Marketing (X01.07.08)

Milk and Dairy Products (X01.07.11)

Fruitgrowing (X01.09.00)

Horticulture-Flowers (X01.10.07)

Shrubs (X01.10.08)

Vegetables (X01.10.09)

or all publications (except Statutory Instruments) on

Pigs (X01.11.16)

Sheep (X01.11.15)

Poultry (X01.11.17)

Rabbits (X01.11.18)

Cattle (X01.11.19)

and, of course, all Agriculture Bulletins (X01.04.12)

If you would like to place a Standing Order for future publications on any of these subjects, call or write to us at one of the Government Bookshops listed on the reverse of the title page of this book (London mail to PO Box 569, London, SE1 9NH). Quote your HMSO Account No. and the classification code of the subject required; if you do not have an Account with HMSO, a deposit of £10 is required for this service. Leaflets are available on how to open an HMSO Account and on the HMSO Standing Order Service.

 **HMSO BOOKS**

Printed in England for Her Majesty's Stationery Office by Staples Printers Kettering Limited at The George Press, Kettering Northamptonshire.
Dd. 595462 K80 9/78